ONLINE BRANDING

Keith Drew

Laurence King Publishing

contents

INTRODUCTION   p.4

WEBSITE: www.absolut.com
DESIGNED BY: Springtime   p.12

WEBSITE: www.adobe.com
DESIGNED BY: Hillman Curtis   p.20

WEBSITE: www.bang-olufsen.com
DESIGNED BY: In-house   p.26

WEBSITE: www.banja.com
DESIGNED BY: Team cHmAn   p.34

WEBSITE: www.billabong-usa.com
DESIGNED BY: Juxt Interactive   p.40

WEBSITE: www.bp.com
DESIGNED BY: Scient   p.48

WEBSITE: www.conran.co.uk
DESIGNED BY: Deepend   p.56

WEBSITE: www.guardian.co.uk
DESIGNED BY: In-house   p.64

WEBSITE: www.guinnessstorehouse.com
DESIGNED BY: Imagination   p.70

WEBSITE: www.habitat.net
DESIGNED BY: Digit   p.78

WEBSITE: www.eu.levi.com
DESIGNED BY: Good Technology   p.86

WEBSITE: www.mercedes-benz.co.uk
DESIGNED BY: Rufus Leonard   p.94

WEBSITE: www.m-three.com
DESIGNED BY: Paris France   p.102

WEBSITE: www.nationalgeographic.com/pearlharbor
DESIGNED BY: Second Story   p.108

WEBSITE: www.nikewomen.com
DESIGNED BY: Framfab   p.116

WEBSITE: www.volkswagenasia.com
DESIGNED BY: Bluewave Singapore   p.124

WEBSITE: www.wallpaper.com
DESIGNED BY: I-D Media   p.130

WEBSITE: www.wmteam.de
DESIGNED BY: WM Team   p.138

GUIDE TO ONLINE BRANDING
                                                      p.144

THE FUTURE OF BRAND DEVELOPMENT
                                                      p.150

When Neil Armstrong and Buzz Aldrin completed the American Apollo 11 mission of walking on the moon, the first thing that greeted them on their return was a neon advertising sign. It simply read: Welcome back to Earth, home of Coca-Cola. (See "Brandwatching: Lifting the Lid on the Phenomenon of Branding", written by Giles Lury and published by Blackhall Publishing, 2001.)

The impact of branding on our society has been enormous. Everyday, people make conscious decisions to eat, drink, buy or wear particular products or labels, often purely because of a corporation's self-projected image. Brands and branding surround us. So, what is branding and where has it come from? Branding, in all its shapes and forms, comes down to how an organization presents itself and, more importantly, how its audience perceives it. It has grown beyond a simple visual depiction into more of an attitude, enforced through

a series of interactions a person has with any one organization.

Branding has a long and varied past. Trademarks have been protecting property and produce for over 8,000 years, while the first branded product was introduced to us by Julius Caesar and co. The branding phenomenon has evolved and grown ever since — the Internet is just the newest medium through which corporations can reach the consumer. However, for the first time in history, a medium now has the potential to deliver a company's identity in seconds. As a result, it affords businesses a whole new way of gaining customers, or losing them. The number of consumers who make purchasing decisions online is growing exponentially. Provide a positive experience for your users and they'll be back. Confuse them, frustrate them, or fail to meet their needs and they'll click onto a competitor's site before you can say "Boo".

In the US alone, the branding industry is worth over $2 trillion. As more and more companies look to the Internet to enhance the relationship between their brand and their consumers, the Internet's role becomes more and more important. It is Web designers who hold the key to success in online branding. Knowing how to express a brand successfully online is a vital part of Web design today — every project corporate designers take on involves some sort of brand development, whether it's creating a brand, refocusing it or conveying it across a number of very different global regions. There are over 70 billion pages on the Internet and users need to have a point they can trust. The point they can trust is the brand.

Opinion over the Web's effect on branding is divided. A lot of cross-media and Web design agencies hold the view that while the Web has brought about changes in the way we conduct commerce and research information, the branding of

0046780RE

When Neil Armstrong and Buzz Aldrin completed the American
Apollo 11 mission of walking on the moon, the first thing
that greeted them on their return was a neon advertising sign.
It simply read: Welcome back to Earth, home of Coca-Cola

Good online branding is
only achievable if you
fully understand the medium
you're working with

products and services remains essentially the same. "Branding is branding; whether it's online, offline, on the radio or on TV, there are basically the same principles guiding the whole thing," says Neil Svensson, co-founder of UK-based brand design consultancy Rufus Leonard. "It's about being able to establish a set of values and a set of behaviours that support your brand and making sure that everyone experiences this. The Web is just another way of communicating with your audience."

It's a view supported by Levi Strauss Europe's Internet marketing manager, Anne Bonew. "I have a hard time thinking of online branding as being any different from any other type of branding: a great idea remains a great idea, regardless of the medium you use to communicate it," she says.

The essence of branding itself hasn't changed that much from its offline predecessor. It continues to revolve around differentiation and trust. However, the way we approach it has changed. In many ways the Internet has proved to be the best bridge between brands and the consumer — it's by far the cheapest and easiest way for companies to communicate with their customer base; you can reach more people in less time, and the brand experience can now be so much more three-dimensional. "The Web has definitely altered the way we approach branding," says Charlie O'Shields, creative director of US-based agency lookandfeel. "Branding involves not only visual design, but also an emotional connection with the target market. With print, there's a very static connection with the individual. Television makes a more emotional connection possible, but the Web gives the user the opportunity to actually interact with brands on a personal level. The ability

of websites to create a community enables brands to not only reach their target markets, but also to bring them together and enable individuals to interact with each other." ABSOLUT Vodka is a case in point. Its latest research has shown that people who visit its website, www.absolut.com, have a stronger relationship with the brand than those who purely enjoy the drinking side of ABSOLUT.

Either way, both parties share one belief — that good online branding is only achievable if you fully understand the medium you're working with. "You have to ensure that your ideas are optimised for the medium," says Anne Bonew. "Nowadays, every brand manager and agency has to ask themselves, 'How do I express this message best on TV, in print, on the radio and on the Internet.'"

For example, completely replicating an offline

brochure online, a practice that peppered the Web during its early days and has refused to go away ever since, ignores the Internet's unique applications. "Online branding offers companies a chance to connect with their consumers on a new level," says Charlie O'Shields. "They can bring everything in their brand arsenal together for their audiences. Companies that create little more than brochure-ware produce a very stale experience for the user that actually gives them less in brand appeal than offline examples."

Understanding the medium is one thing. Understanding the mindset needed to express a brand's core is a different skill altogether. In 1931, a designer at Coca-Cola's headquarters in Atlanta was asked to design a Coke bottle that had such a strong identity that if you smashed it into hundreds of little pieces and picked up just one, then you'd still be able to recognize it as the Coke brand. No logo. No name. Just

strong design that captured the essence of the brand.

In recent years, there's been a misleading notion that branding is all about a company's graphic symbol or logo. Plaster your logo across the site enough times and everything will work out fine. The "look and feel" of a site is certainly an important aspect of branding, but it's just one ingredient. Branding makes up the entire user experience — it's every aspect of the relationship between the company and the consumer. As companies seek to build and develop their brands online, they are entering a completely new arena. "Companies are moving beyond logos, taglines and graphic identity and into the customer's total experience of interacting with the brand," says Robert Manning of UK-based Agency.com.

Logos and taglines are effective only in that they summarize the attitude of an organization. They support the brand but they don't

create it. Branding culminates in a symbol that people associate with an experience they've had with an organization, but the hard work of branding goes into making that experience. "Strong branding has nothing to do with a beautiful logo, but it has everything to do with your brand's message," says Martin Lindstrom, CEO of Danish agency Digitas and author of Brand Building on the Internet. "What do you want your brand to say? What tracks should it leave in the consumer's mind after exposure to it? What are its values?"

A lot of this work will be dictated by the role the brand plays in people's lives. Far too many dotcom brands made the mistake of assuming their service instantly formed an integral part of people's lives. They overestimated their own importance and paid the price. In more successful examples, when Juxt Interactive created a site for Billabong, the surfing

Branding culminates in a symbol that people
associate with an experience they've had
with an organization, but the hard work of
branding goes into making that experience

Consumers build brands
like birds build nests —
from the scraps and straws
they chance upon

company's hardcore audience dictated that the site should focus 100 percent on the brand. When Framfab Australia developed a site for Libra, a feminine-hygiene product, the context of that commodity decreed that the agency tone the branding down. As an advisory website, Libra would have been deemed far less impartial had it tried to come on strong with the branding. In both cases, the brand's role dictated the site's level of branding.

The constant in both of the latter examples is the audience. Supplying consumers with exactly what they need is a core issue of branding. If your website fulfils user expectations or better, then people will leave the site knowing that the brand with which they have just interacted has provided a relevant and welcome service to their everyday lives. "Meeting users' needs is the one thing that gets missed a lot in branding," says Juxt Interactive's Todd Purgason. "People spin off these crazy viral marketing campaigns for a brand that are just over-embellished newspaper adverts, whereas

the Internet's really about providing people with information and experiences that they just can't get anywhere else." Juxt Interactive recently added an online shop to the site it created for Billabong (www.billabong-usa.com) to meet a strong user need. "The site's branding was coming off and it had lots of interactive content, but people were interested in the gear," says Todd. "They wanted to shop, and that wasn't there. Although visually and attitude-wise, we were presenting a really strong brand online, it was falling down to a certain extent because we weren't meeting the audience's needs."

Juxt Interactive corrected the site and added a useful customer service to an already powerfully branded experience. It's a classic case of addressing the needs of a specific audience, and shows the importance of understanding how to successfully express a brand in Web design today. As Web designers know, every corporate project they ever deal with involves some form

of brand development. The aim of this book is to take an in-depth look at how a range of the very best professional Web design agencies, from the UK, Europe, Asia and the US have tackled different aspects of branding in their respective projects. Big-name sites such as BP, Guinness, Habitat, Levi's, Nike and Mercedes-Benz deal with such themes as developing an online brand, refocusing and rebranding, conveying a variant brand message and delivering a multinational brand to very different global regions.

The following projects will give an insight into the inspiration and creative process behind some exceptionally well-branded sites. Branding is very important. Outside of its pure monetary value to Web agencies, branding is shaping a lot of the work Web designers currently do. Jeremy Bullmore, of US advertising company JWT, once said, "Consumers build brands like birds build nests — from the scraps and straws they chance upon." It's time to do the building for them.

www.absolut.com

CLIENT: Absolut

DESIGNED BY: Springtime

DEVELOPMENT TIME: 1 year

SIZE OF PROJECT TEAM: 3—8 people, varying over time

TECHNOLOGY USED: Flash, HTML and Shockwave

CONTACT: www.springtime.se

"Our latest site still intends to make our users think. You must never underestimate your consumer's intelligence. Underestimate your consumer, and they'll only underestimate your brand"

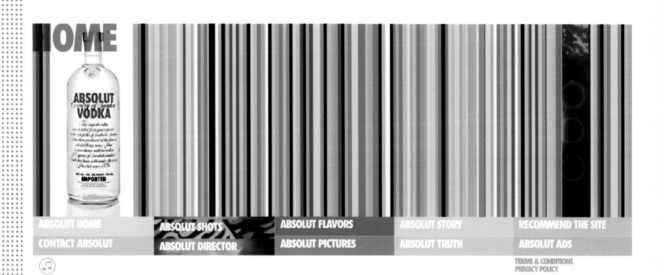

ABSOLUT·IS·A·BRAND·THAT·LIKES·TO·DO·THINGS
DIFFERENTLY.·ITS·LATEST·SITE·USES·A·VARIETY·OF
TECHNIQUES·TO·CONTINUE·ITS·ONLINE·CREATIVITY

ABSOLUT Vodka likes to take an alternative
approach. Its new exploratory navigation system
guides users through its site.

ABSOLUT, the leading
Vodka manufacturer, has
established itself as a
creative and witty brand, the
kind of brand you'd like to
have in your drinks cabinet.
It's a lifestyle brand, but
one that has set itself up
as taking an alternative
approach, and its website
reflects this positioning
perfectly.

"The ABSOLUT philosophy is
to never do what everyone
else does," says Christina
Bergman, ABSOLUT's Internet
communications manager.
"We've avoided banner ads
for a long time, but we saw
an opportunity to poke fun
at the format and its
infamous drawbacks. As the
medium has grown — and grown
up — we thought it was time
for an ABSOLUT twist on
online advertising." ABSOLUT
LIMITATIONS, a tongue-in-
cheek media-specific
commentary on the pitfalls of
online advertising, was born.

ABSOLUT has never pursued the
traditional advertising route
online in the past. Instead,
its strategy has been to

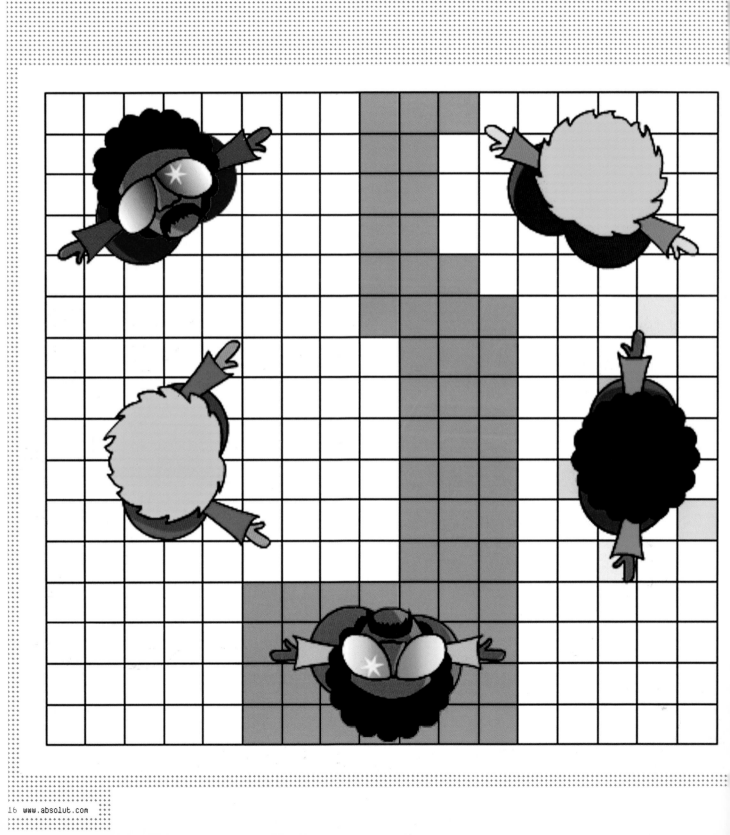

support the Internet by providing cutting-edge interactive entertainment content, and giving branding very much a back-seat role. The essence of each of the websites in ABSOLUT's colourful history has been to focus on a lifestyle aspect, be it art, illustration, music or film. In 1996, it launched ABSOLUT KELLY, the first of its experimental sites and a complete contrast to its competitors' more general creations that

targeted a broader audience. Kevin Kelly's vision of futuristic art was a classic example of ABSOLUT's aim of focusing on the Web's early adopters by creating cutting-edge projects. ABSOLUT KELLY was followed a year later by ABSOLUT PANUSHKA, featuring animations from Christine Panushka, and then in 1998 by ABSOLUT DJ, a music-focused website with DJ Spooky. ABSOLUT DIRECTOR, a Shockwave application that enables you to script, edit and score

your own short film and zooms across the current site as a link, was a natural step from music and extended the company's ownership of creative content online. Among the site's technical feats, it has the first text-to-speech engine that enables users to generate their own spoken dialogue in the film.

The Internet's widespread adoption has seen ABSOLUT change its online aims. The vodka firm decided that its

PRESS ROOM

ABSOLUT HOME   CLOSE ABSOLUT.COM

ABSOLUT HOLLEIN.

new site should appeal to all
its target groups — users
interested in the Web
experience, 'brand fans' and
anyone in search of a premium
tipple. It is still committed
to creating cutting-edge
work, though. The user
interface creates a powerful
expression of sound and
vision that works on several
platforms, and the site
displays itself in a full-
screen window to avoid visual
interference from other
elements on the computer
desktop.

"Our latest site <absolut.com>
still intends to make our
users think," says Christina.
"We aimed to develop an
informative site about the
most coveted vodka brand in
the world in a thought-
provoking and creative way,
and to do this it was
important to provide our
users with some unexpected
content. You must never
underestimate your consumer's
intelligence. It was this
communication principle that
governed our exploratory
navigation system on the new
site. Underestimate your
consumer, and they'll only
underestimate your brand."

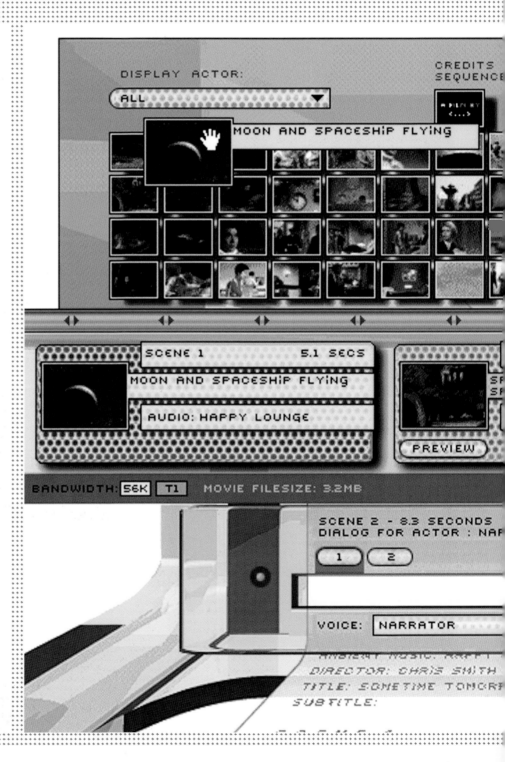

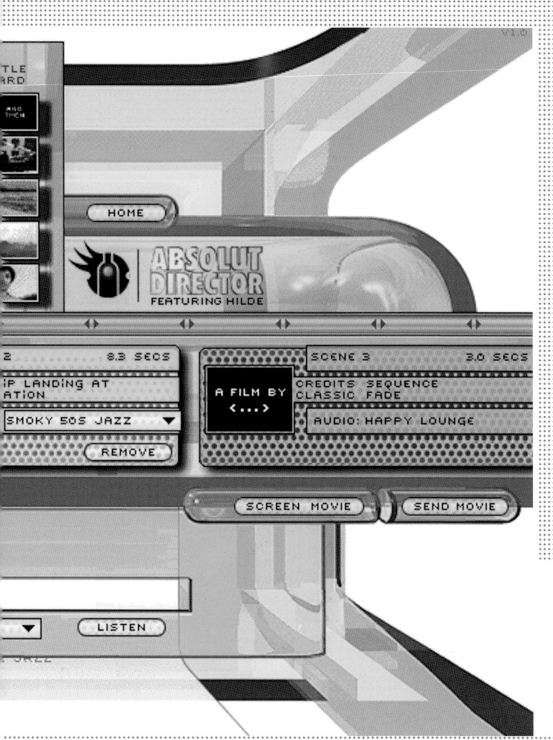

V1.0

TLE
RD

ANO
THEN.

HOME

ABSOLUT
DIRECTOR
FEATURING HILDE

2   8.3 SECS   SCENE 3   3.0 SECS

iP LANDING AT   A FILM BY   CREDITS SEQUENCE
ATION   < ... >   CLASSIC FADE

SMOKY 50S JAZZ   ▼   AUDIO: HAPPY LOUNGE

REMOVE

SCREEN MOVIE   SEND MOVIE

▼   LISTEN

Following on from ABSOLUT DJ,
ABSOLUT DIRECTOR is a Shockwave
application that enables you to script,
edit and score your own short film.

www.adobe.com

CLIENT: Adobe

DESIGNED BY: Hillman Curtis

DEVELOPMENT TIME: 2 ¹/₂ months

SIZE OF PROJECT TEAM: 5 people

TECHNOLOGY USED: GoLive, Illustrator, ImageReady and Photoshop

CONTACT: www.hillmancurtis.com

"One of a website's main tasks
is to communicate; another is
to respect its audience. You
have to take a visual picture
of your audience and
cater to their needs"

 Adobe
everywhere
you look™

Store   Products   Support   Corporate   Adobe Studio | Search | Contact us

 Acrobat 5.0 video tour
Find out how to review within a
browser, use online forms, and
more.

**Photoshop wins
Web Techniques
Readers' Choice Award**

One of "the most innovative
products in the Web development
process."

 **What's new in
Illustrator 10**
Extraordinary creative freedom

Now with native support for Mac
OS X and Microsoft Windows XP.

 **Howard
Schatz**
photography
that defies
gravity.

Adobe Studio✿™

 InDesign 2.0
Capture your inspiration and
publish it anywhere – in print, on
the Web, and more.

 Adobe DesignTeam
Conduct online reviews, share
files, and track projects. Free
30-day trial.

🛒 **Adobe Store** ›
Other ways to buy

📺 **web** ›
High-impact Web design and
publishing

print ›
From desktop to paper to Web

digital video ›
For film, multimedia, and the
Web

digital imaging ›
World-class tools for digital
photographers

ePaper ›
Acrobat solutions and
eBooks   Adobe PDF

Adobe announces

· Try Adobe.com on your PDA
· Special: Adobe Web Collection and
  IBM® IntelliStation®
· Individual type styles now available
  in Adobe Store
· Adobe and Mac OS X
  Free e-mail newsletters
  Press Room

Training ›
Events ›
Adobe in Education ›
Partner programs ›

HILLMAN·CURTIS·WORKED·CLOSELY·WITH·ADOBE·TO
CREATE·A·SITE·THAT·APPEALED·BOTH·TO·THE·WEB
DESIGN·COMMUNITY·AND·TO·THE·AVERAGE·HOME·USER

Adobe is synonymous with Web design. Its range of products, such as GoLive, Illustrator and Photoshop, have shaped the Internet's look and enabled designers to push their individual projects. Having such an important role, the software company's own site serves as a hub, a place where Web designers converge to find out the latest news and swap technology tips.

When New York-based agency Hillman Curtis Inc. took on the site's redesign, the first thing it sought to express was this interconnection of Adobe with the design community. "We used a ring metaphor to illustrate this aspect of the brand and, while the rings don't actually intersect, there's always one in the background that's tying them all together," says Hillman Curtis, the agency's company director. It's a concatenating theme that extends to Adobe's tools as well. "It's very important for any software company with a suite of tools to communicate to its audience that all these tools work together seamlessly," says Hillman.

Adobe everywhere you look™

Store   Products   Support   ▸ Corporate

About Adobe   Press
Community   Contact A

about Adobe

"*Good ideas come from everywhere in the company.*"
John Warnock
Chairman and Founder

Founded in 1982, Adobe Sy
solutions for Network Pub
broadband applications. Its
authoring tools enable cus
content for various types o
graphic designers, profess
business users, and consu
in the U.S., with annual re
employees worldwide and
Rim, Japan, and Latin Ame
California.

*Adobe's vision: Netw
Publish anything, ar*

The enormous amount of information on the new Adobe website had to be expressed in a clearer and more tangible way than the original site had managed.

Adobe Studio | Search | Contact us

nvestors   Adobe Ventures

corporated builds award-winning software
including Web, print, video, wireless, and
design, imaging, dynamic media, and
create, publish, and deliver visually rich
The company's products are used by Web and
lishers, document-intensive organizations,
be is the second largest PC software company
xceeding $1.2 billion. It employs over 2,800
tions in North America, Europe, the Pacific
be's worldwide headquarters are in San Jose,

ublishing
e, on any device.
more ▶

What marks adobe.com out from other corporate websites is the sheer amount of information it contains. Hillman Curtis had to express this in a clearer and more tangible way than the original site had managed. "The war cry for the redesign was 'creative and easy' — a direct reflection of Adobe's reputation as a software company," he says. Other than helping to visually prioritize the information, one of the biggest challenges of the redesign was taking what Hillman refers to as "the unworkable global navigation" of the original site and turning it into something more functional. "We designed this wonderfully simple global navigation system that consists of just four words," he says. "The original nav worked OK, but it would appear differently throughout the site and, in this medium, the rule is consistency."

Although adobe.com sits at the hub of an online Web design community, the site appeals to people outside this sector. A significant proportion of Adobe's customers are the normal folk who come looking for Acrobat Reader. "One of a website's main tasks is to communicate;

another is to respect its audience. You have to take a visual picture of your audience and cater to their needs," says Hillman. "We had to make the site simple enough to service the needs of the millions of people who come to Adobe just for the Acrobat plug-in; people who don't care about Photoshop tricks, or what Matt Owens' latest creation looks like. We had to grind it all together and come out with a really simple, functional — yet creative — design."

Fulfilling the brief was made easier for Hillman Curtis Inc. by the agency's intrinsic relationship with Adobe. It's important to know your brand inside out, and working closely with the client is one of the best ways of doing this. It definitely worked for Hillman Curtis. "We were able to create a really strong bond of collaboration with Adobe, and it turned out to be one of the best experiences I've had working with another creative team," he says. "It's something that we try to do with every client, but we just hit it off with Adobe."

The Adobe redesign uses a ring metaphor to express the interconnection of the company's tools and the interlinking of Adobe with the design community.

Tomato | FEATURE | GALLERY

April 2001

📺 View the QuickTime movie

◀   view gallery   ▶

Dawn of Man
This group of clips comes from a series of reconstructions of the life of early man
put together for the BBC documentary "Ape Man." Tomato was tasked to produce
six short films that portrayed key moments in human history. Here, you can find
an amalgam of all of them.

Shot in South Africa in late 1999, the short films are an excellent example of the
lush style of Graham Wood and Dirk van Dooren. Much of Wood's personal work
incorporates this kind of slow-moving, beautiful shooting.

www.bang-olufsen.com

CLIENT: Bang & Olufsen
DESIGNED BY: Inhouse
DEVELOPMENT TIME: 4 months
SIZE OF PROJECT TEAM: 4 people
TECHNOLOGY USED: HTML, Flash and php
CONTACT: www.bang-olufsen.com

"We wanted to create our own
space that hasn't been designed
in the usual way. Many people
will perceive this as us taking
a standpoint, and that's
exactly what we want"

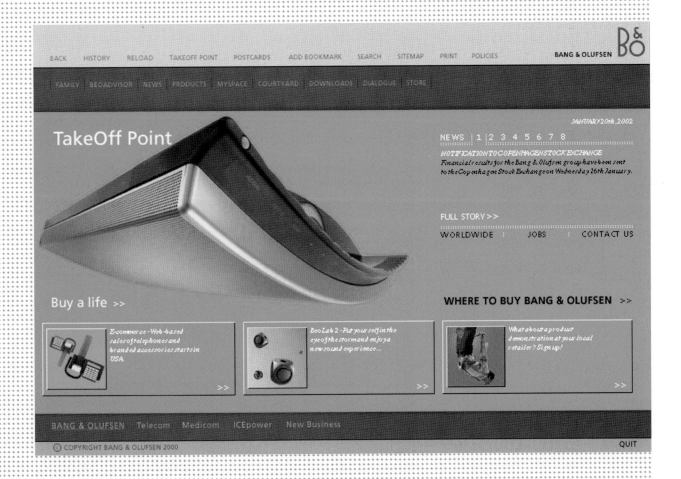

BANG ▪ & ▪ OLUFSEN'S ▪ INHOUSE ▪ TEAM ▪ COMBINED ▪ DESIGN, CONTENT, ▪ DYNAMICS ▪ AND ▪ STABILITY ▪ TO ▪ TRANSFER ▪ ITS STRONG ▪ OFFLINE ▪ INDIVIDUALITY ▪ ONTO ▪ THE ▪ WEB

A Bang & Olufsen hi-fi stands out because it is different. The sleek design and unusual shape almost disguise the fact that it's a hi-fi at all. This uniqueness is inherent in the company's ethos, and it's a characteristic that its inhouse Web team was keen to transfer online.

"It's the one thing that makes us who we are," says Dorthe Høj Jensen at Bang & Olufsen. "People often have to get used to our products before they accept them, but then they go on to become part of their lives. With the Web, we wanted to create our own space that wasn't designed in the usual way. Many people will perceive this as us taking a standpoint, and that's exactly what we want."

The "space" that Bang & Olufsen created expands full-screen across your monitor

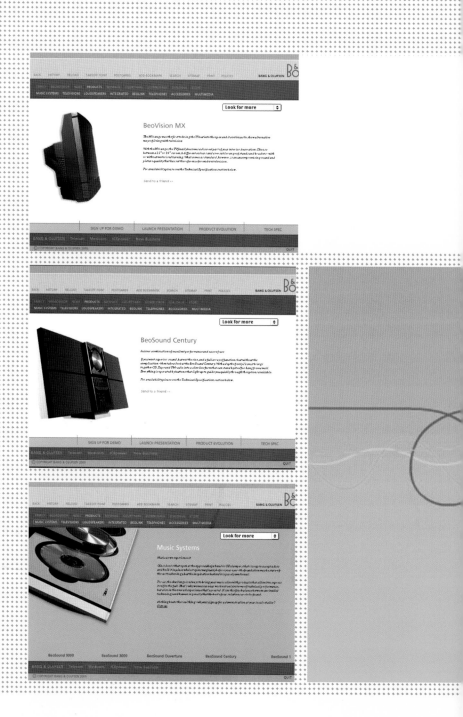

The Bang & Olufsen website attempts to strike a
balance between design and content, dynamics and
stability – and succeeds.

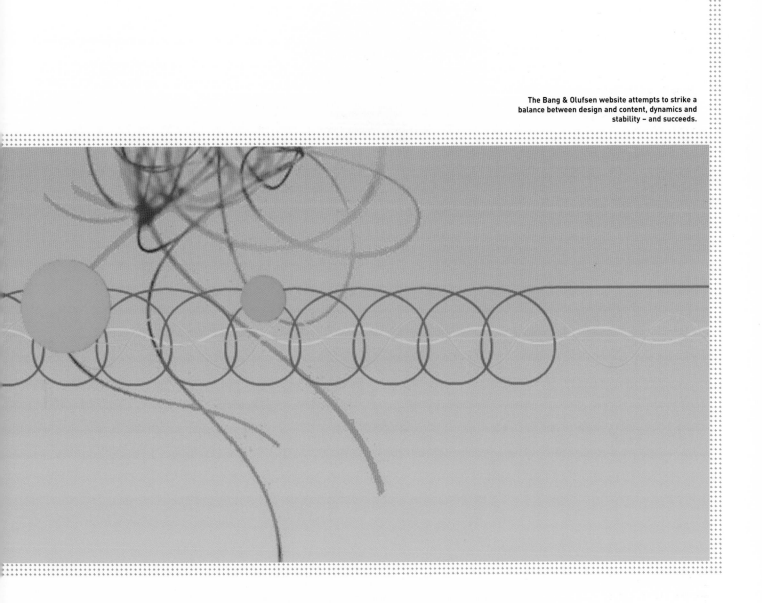

and contains information,
news, advice and pop-up Flash
product presentations. "Full
screen enables our users to
forget the outside world for
a few minutes and immerse
themselves within the scene
we set," says Dorthe. The
focus, as with Bang &
Olufsen's video products, is
on viewing comfort. "We want
to greet the people who join
our world, and create peace
and calm around the experience
that they're about to have."

The site is designed to cater
for both first-time users and
the more dedicated Bang &
Olufsen aficionados. First-
time users can view an entry
page before each section that
sets the mood, then scan the
content or read it in detail.
Long-term users, who are more
familiar with the site, can
navigate solely through the
main menu.

Despite moving away from
colours in the offline world,
the Web team placed a strong
emphasis on using colours to

PRODUCTVIEW

PRODUCTS E-STORE POSTCARDS COURTYARD MYSPA

Wallpaper

Please choose the wallpaper you wish to
download from the list below.

☐ BeoVision 3   ☐ BeoSound 3000   ☐ BeoCenter 1

INTERNATIONAL   **NORTH**AMERICA   STORELOCATO

WNLOADS   CONTACT US   BEOTIME

Look for more ⬍

The focus of the Bang & Olufsen site, as with its
video products, is on viewing comfort.

BeoSound 9000   ▫ BeoLab 2   ▫ BeoSound 1

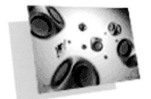

Next

PRESSROOM   RECRUITMENT   BUSINESSMAGAZINE

QUIT

create the right moods and impressions on the site. As Dorthe explains: "Blue stands for intelligence and is therefore used in our product section. Green is a relaxing colour, and is used in close and personal communications with our users, like in the 'BeoAdvisor' and contact sections, whereas we use red in 'My Space' because it's a colour that's close to your heart. It's your life."

Above all, there's a real balance between design and content, dynamics and stability on the Bang & Olufsen site. It's a hard balance to create, but one the inhouse team has managed to carry off well. "The relationship between these four components should articulate the brand," says Dorthe. "In this space, we need to define ourselves." The balance Bang & Olufsen has achieved continues to reflect its offline individuality.

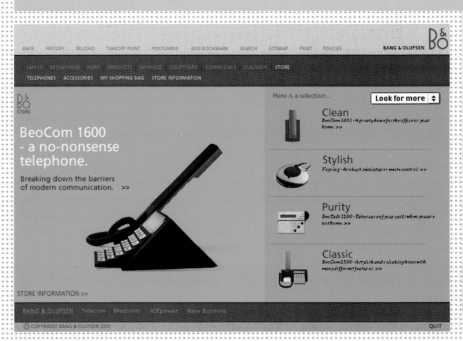

OWNLOADS   CONTACT US   BEOTIME

Look for more ⬍

Classic Products

www.banja.com

SITE: Banja

DESIGNED BY: Team cHmAn

DEVELOPMENT TIME: 2 years

SIZE OF PROJECT TEAM: 15 people

TECHNOLOGY USED: 3DSMax, BWIPI and Flash

CONTACT: www.chman.com

"Banja equals community. We used
all the communication tools
normally associated with the Web,
such as email, news and message
forums, to help people learn how
to live together"

HAVING ESTABLISHED COMMUNITY AS THE ESSENCE OF ITS BRAND, TEAM CHMAN LOOKED TO COMPLETELY ABSORB ITS USERS IN BANJA

Team cHmAn's own cinematic production tool, the BWIPI, totally immerses users in the game as they guide their little Rastafarian player across Itland.

Team cHmAn focused the Banja brand around community and communication. The site uses email, news, message forums and other tools to help bring people together.

Internet start-ups have enjoyed a mixed success. Some, such as Amazon and Yahoo!, have quickly established themselves amongst the most powerful brands in the world. Other, equally well-publicized brands have departed more ignominiously. Not tied to translating traditional brand values online, they are, however, faced with the problem of establishing a brand from scratch.

Banja is a monthly, real-time online 3D game that's quickly cultivated a faithful following. Players guide Banja — a little, peace-loving Rastafarian character — through the interactive

environment that constitutes Itland, an imaginary universe where the Banja game is played out.

As a start-up online venture, Team cHmAn needed to give the brand experience a focal point. To make it more than just an online game, cHmAn built Banja around the whole notions of communication and community. "Banja equals community," says Team ChmAn's Damien Junior. "When we first started, we wanted to use Banja as a way of combining the Internet with an ideology. We wanted to use all the communication tools normally associated with the Web, such as email, news and message forums, to help people learn how to live together."

With the essence of its brand established, cHmAn set about developing Banja's community aspect. The key, it soon discovered, was to let the players affect the outcome of the game as much as possible.

"Banja is a fully interactive story; you have to explore Itland, meet people and carry

Banja is a little, peace-loving Rastafarian character, who the player has to guide through the interactive environment that constitutes the imaginary universe of Itland.

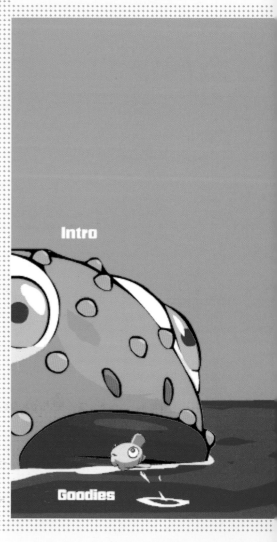

Intro

Goodies

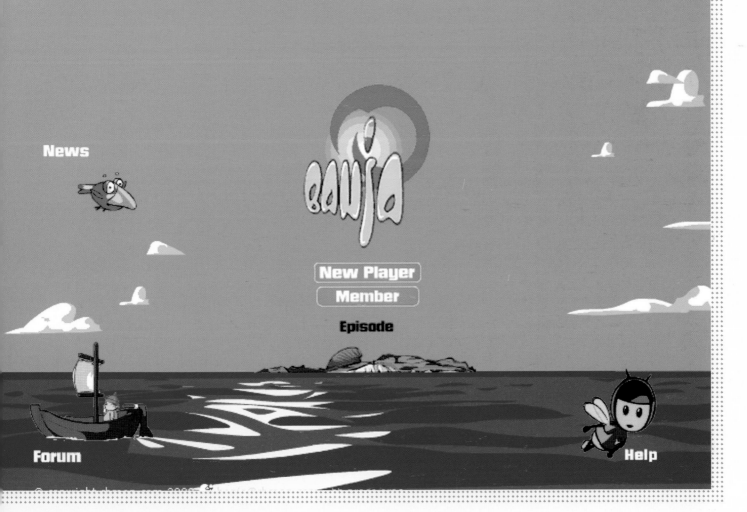

To make the brand experience more than just a game, Team cHmAn built Banja around the notions of communication and community.

out tasks," says Damien. "Players generate the evolution of their own world, through their choices, their knowledge and their behaviour towards the other characters in the game." Involvement is a vital part of the site. Letting players edit Itland's newspaper and delivering regular emails to their desktops has enhanced the brand experience. Players feel that they are constantly part of a much bigger picture. "There are many community activities in Banja and it's very, very important for the players to exchange their ideas and opinions with each other," says Damien.

To totally immerse players in the game, Team cHmAn had to invent its own cinematic production tool. The BWIPI (Banja Work In Progress Interface) tool manages character movements and enables all camera movements, such as zooming and dollying, to be created in Flash. In

the online version, the tool enables the administrator to control all game components on the server.

The feeling of community is compounded by Team cHmAn's use of rhetoric on the site. A new and innovative language was invented specifically for Banja. All dialogue is illustrated by a logical system of sound iconography that can be understood by players all around the world while, equally as important, remaining unintelligible to those who have never played the game.

Damien believes that Banja's popularity stems from its incorporation of real social and moral values, combined with a strong image and peaceful ideology. The Banja community is certainly buying into the brand. Enough, Damien hopes, for them to ease Banja's transition from online game to television series in the coming months.

www.billabong-usa.com

CLIENT: Billabong

DESIGNED BY: Juxt Interactive

DEVELOPMENT TIME: 6 months

SIZE OF PROJECT TEAM: 3 people

TECHNOLOGY USED: Cold fusion, Flash, Generator, HTML, Javascript, Media Cleaner Pro and Quicktime

CONTACT: www.juxt-interactive.com

"In the surfing industry, they can smell a rat. You really need to have an understanding of who the market is and what their culture is about; you have to know what the audience wants"

IMMERSING · ITSELF · IN · THE · CULTURE · HELPED · JUXT INTERACTIVE · REPRESENT · BILLABONG · AS · AN AUTHENTIC · BRAND · WHEN · THE · COMPANY · LOOKED · TO EXPAND · INTO · THE · SNOW · AND · SKATE · SCENE

Surfers and the Internet have been linked ever since the first report of a West Coast swell was published online. Although, being such a tight-knit community, surfing can be a fashion-fickle industry and, as a myriad of surfing companies have moved onto the Internet, only those with the strongest identity have survived.

Australian surfing company Billabong recognized the importance of industry knowledge when it came to develop its new site, Billabong USA. Hailing from the beaches of southern California, Todd Purgason, Juxt Interactive's creative director, grew up in the midst of a surfing culture and has witnessed first hand its changing graphic style. "The surf industry used to be dominated by grunge design — something that resembled a balance between intensity and elegance — but for the last three or four years, the industry's been in this new-school tech mode," he explains. "Billabong thought harder-edged punk was the next trend, and when its people saw our Shorn site [www.shorn.com], its punk style really sparked the company's interest in what it could do with Flash on the Web."

Shorn's visual style helped Juxt get the project, but the agency had more to do than simply instil the Billabong USA site with a graphic attitude. Founded in 1973, Billabong is one of the mainstays of the surfing industry. Its reputation in surfing is unquestionable, but the last five years have seen a massive push in other similar sports. Skateboarding and snowboarding are now more popular than they have ever been, and Billabong was keen to widen its appeal to both communities on its new site. "Expanding the Billabong brand to the skate and snow communities was a big push behind what we were doing," says Todd. "Five years ago, the company probably wouldn't have bothered to make the investment, but this time it was really important that the site be able to support all these individual communities."

Billabong USA was designed to focus primarily on surfing but also included sub-branded sections attuned to their respective audiences: "surf" is fast and edgy, "snow" is designed to represent the more technical nature of snowboarding, while "skate" is, as Todd says, "more raw, more energetic, more street".

billabong SNOW

FEATURE ▶ RIDER

FOOTAGE ▶

TEAM
RIDER
VIDEOS

feature

KEVIN JONES ▶

Budweiser, Ford's
and Kevin Jones

Juxt worked hard to get the tone of each sub-branded section right. Representing an authentic brand is always essential, but it's especially so in the extreme sports arena, where outsiders are found out and quickly. "In this particular industry, they can smell a rat," says Todd. "It's evolving, but there was a time when if you got rejected by the community, you were dead. You'd be out in one season and it would be over. It's not as drastic now, but you still really need to have an understanding of who the market is and what their culture is about; you still have to know what the audience wants."

Unlike other companies that rely on strict branding guidelines, businesses in the extreme sport industry tend to have very flexible brands, re-inventing themselves depending on what trends dictate. Introducing new product lines five times a year, Billabong is in the unique position of virtually redefining itself every ten weeks. "Billabong is really concerned with staying cool

Billabong USA is split into sub-branded sections. "Surf" is fast and edgy, "snow" is more technical, while "skate" is, as Todd says, "more raw, more energetic, more street".

7

NEWS

Team Billabong Brazil's Costa makes the Newport event finals with Taj and Andy.

MORE

Billabong Brazil skateboarder Rodil de Araújo wins his third gold in Philadelphia.

MORE

BILLABONG

with the culture, so that
its products sell, but at
the same time the company is
constantly morphing, so it's
always visually pushing and
progressing," says Todd.

Constant brand evolution
can make it difficult for
agencies to get a solid
understanding of their
client's identity, but Juxt's
core understanding of the
surfing industry countered
this. In fact, Juxt's branding
of Billabong USA has proved
so successful that Billabong
used the site's graphic style
and attitude to develop its
snow and skate brands. Its
surfing brand has also
subsequently pulled from the
Pickled site 〖www.pickled.tv〗
additional Juxt work that
appears as a link on the
Billabong USA homepage. "The
essence of it is the energy
and the attitude," says Todd.
"If you're just selling and
presenting content, people
are going to see through that
and it's not going to make a
connection. And you need to
make that connection. You
need to ask yourself what
your audience is looking for,
what they need and how you
can use the Internet to
supply that need."

www.bp.com

CLIENT: BP
DESIGNED BY: Scient
DEVELOPMENT TIME: 6 months
SIZE OF PROJECT TEAM: 30+ people
TECHNOLOGY USED: Flash, HomeSite, Illustrator and Photoshop
CONTACT: www.scient.com

"The global style guide is a blueprint of everything you need to construct your site. It sets out everything from content standards, graphic icons and language style guides, to how to create your information architecture"

bp

deep-sea intelligence

seabed survey vehicle
has its own 'brain'

A new kind of unmanned submarine that operates independently is being used for deep-sea surveys in the Gulf of Mexico.

next ▶

SCIENT·DEVELOPED·A·GLOBAL·STYLE·GUIDE·FOR BP'S·NEW·SITE·TO·ENABLE·THE·COMPANY·TO SPEAK·WITH·ONE·BRAND,·ONE·VOICE

BP was in the midst of a rebranding process when it contracted Scient to relaunch bp.com as its new catch-all portal. A complex system of multinationals, the scale of BP's global business made the task facing Scient a pretty unique one. BP includes many separate companies like Amoco, ARCO and Burmah Castrol and, when Scient took on the project, it found the whole set-up very fragmented. Each of these companies had its own site door. Combined with the various regional offices, there were more than 160 sites representing different facets of BP on the Web.

"The challenge was to address all these different sites around the world," says Tomas Ancona, a creative strategist at Scient. "They wanted BP to speak with one brand and one voice, so our objective was to create a central portal that could speak to the corporate communications channel folk, engage customers and move people smoothly across the various businesses."

Scient's role was to design and build a new parent site and to establish a global style guide that would be used to relaunch the other sites around the world. The style guide sets out the design guidelines used on the main bp.com site, and offers advice on implementing the corporation's brand values. "It's a blueprint of everything you need to construct your site," says Tomas. "It sets out the design rules for the individual businesses to work with — from content standards, graphic icons and language style guides, to how to create your information architecture." Scient created a very simple and elegant navigation system — a series of cascading menus that tells people how deep to go with each layer — which has become a standard for all the independent businesses, as well as commissioning a photo shoot that now sits at the heart of the look and feel it created.

Newsletter
Programme news and
project achievements

the bp conser

| about us | news | a |

Providing support to stude
projects world-wide.

| conservation home | bp.com | investor |

LEGAL NOTICE | contact us

© 1999-2001 BP p.l.c.

·n programme

projects | applications

**2002 Conservation
Programme Winners**

- Follow-up winner: Kikuyu
  Escarpment Outreach -
  community involvement in
  Kenya.
- Gold Winner: Urugua-i
  Green Corridor -
  conserving a green corridor
  in Argentina
- Gold Winner: Proyecto
  Hapalopsittaca. Parrots in
  the Colombian Andes
- Gold Winner: CROC -
  Community Research,
  Observance &
  Conservation in the
  Philippines

conservation

press centre | career centre

Privacy statement

Scient addressed the discontinuity of BP's range of sites around the world by designing
a global style guide that set out the design guidelines used on the main bp.com site, and
by offering advice on implementing the corporation's brand values.

Ultimately, though, the sites connected to bp.com are owned by their individual businesses. Worried that an overly restrictive set of rules would turn designers off, Scient developed the branding style guide along a theme it called "flexibility in the right places" — a global standard that provides an open set of design systems that people can work within. "It's pretty exciting to see the variety within the sites that have been built already," says Tomas. "BP Greece, for example, has clearly got the right look and feel, but with its own distinct personality."

The exploding logos and varying navigation systems that made up BP's previous external sites are a thing of the past. Scient has calmed down the design, treated the logo with respect and restrained the use of green that once dominated the network. The biggest change, though, is the main site's attitude to its audience. BP's wish to engage its customers as a brand has seen the portal's focus shift.

"The aim was to change it from a business-centric site to a user-centric site," says

◀ style guide

bp

Welcome
One brand, one voice
BP's values
Energy for life
Design principles
Customer-centric
bp.com home page
Transition pages
Navigation
BP site home pages
Summary

Energy for life

The emphasis of bp.com has shifted away
from big business towards the consumer.
Real-life stories of BP employees help
enhance brand positioning.

cleaner fuels for the journey ahead

Choose your country:

Cleaner fuels
for the journey ahead

Can you have
mobility and
clean air?

Tomas. "The homepage is really about the customer; we've moved the focus from BP talking about itself and its businesses to what people need when they get to the front door." The ways that people come into the site — into a corporate channel, a business that they know, a country portal, or an industry sector — now gives them everything they might need that relates to their role in the industry.

But the new consumer-centric side of BP doesn't stop there. Scient created a series of 12 interactive stories about BP that help bring the brand to life. Featuring anecdotes of community involvement, technological innovations and environmental projects from people across the company, the story section represents the company's brand values without shouting about them at the front door. "Your brand is your story; it's who you are," says Tomas. "If you can sit there and tell your story, then that's essentially the best expression of your brand. We try and get people to tell stories."

bp

Find out the latest information about BP, our performance and policies

our businesses

in yo

our company

meeting your needs

bp

Find out the latest information about BP, our performance and policies

our company

our businesses

in your area

2001: BP Brings Clean Buses To The Streets O

Download our new annual report

Find out more about our Annual General Meeting and electronic voting

Serving aviation customers around the world. Visit AirBP to find out more

meeting your needs

checking the sand

new detection practices benefit cost, safety and the environment

| bp.com home | investor centre | press centre | career centre | energy review |

bp

Πμ?ρα Περιβ?λλοντος
Φερ?ντας γ?νεται και καπ?λα

Οδικ? Ασφ?λεια
?παινοι για τη BP Hellas

Ο Πλίος της BP
Ν?α αφ?νιση στα Πρατ?ρια

καλώς ήλθατε στην bp hellas

εταιρία   εξυπηρετώντας σας   κοινωνία   περιβάλλον

καινοτόμος

→ προοδευτική

→ καθαρή

→ πράσινη

EN
Click here for english language

Η σημεριν? BP ε?ναι μια ν?α εταιρ?α. Μια εταιρ?α με ν?ες Προσεγγ?σεις, ?ναν ν?ο τρ?πο σκ?ψης, απ?λυτα ανοιχτ? σε ν?ες δυνατ?τητες. Ως ενεργειακ? επιχε?ρηση με ηγετικ? θ?ση παγκοσμ?ως, παρ?χουμε στους καταναλωτ?ς τη δυνατ?τητα να μετακινηθο?ν, να αντιμετωπ?σουν τις κλιματικ?ς συνθ?κες, τη δυνατ?τητα να απολα?σουν μια καλ?τερη ποι?τητα ζω?ς.

www.conran.co.uk

CLIENT: Conran

DESIGNED BY: Deepend

DEVELOPMENT TIME: 7 months

SIZE OF PROJECT TEAM: 14 people

TECHNOLOGY USED: EJB, HTML, Java, JSP, Photoshop and XML

"It often comes secondary to design, but the tone of the copy is just as important. Talking to someone in the wrong way online can severely damage your brand"

EAT SHOP LIVE US

HOME

A-Z OF RESTAURANTS
INSPIRE ME
ONLINE BOOKING
PRIVATE DINING
CONRAN CARD
SPECIAL OFFERS

JOBS

Conran
Cooking

Welcome to Eat

Eat is for lovers of good food and wine. Whether you want to book a table on-line in one of the Conran restaurants, check out our menus, or just be inspired - Eat is for you.

Our restaurants and shops are filled with people who are passionate about food and drink, we hope you will join us. Bon voyage or should we say bon appetit.

DEEPEND USED A CLEAN STYLE AND A
SIMPLE APPROACH TO BRING TOGETHER
CONRAN'S MANY BUSINESS FACETS

eat

shop

live

us

A-Z OF RESTAURANTS
INSPIRE ME
ONLINE BOOKING
PRIVATE DINING
SPECIAL OFFERS

" Attention to detail
is a good indication
that a place is truly
cared for. "

CONRAN

Say "Conran" to someone in the UK and they'll think of shopping. Or restaurants. Or perhaps furniture. Or maybe even design. Conran is a multi-faceted brand that meets its customers in a variety of contexts.

Its numerous business facets all have very different styles and yet there is something very "Conran" about them all. The agency handed the job of bringing Conran's variant strains together was Deepend, a UK-based agency that, despite creating a variety of award-winning sites, was forced to close down in 2001. "They all have this feeling of something that doesn't date," explains Tony Philips, design director. "Conran always uses the word 'timeless' to describe what it does. It's all in the approach; not everything will look the same or feel the same, but it's still had the same amount of effort put into it."

Creating something with a timeless appeal online is a little hard. With the ever-changing world of the Web, you're lucky to even have your site looking fresh come launch time. Adhering to Conran's wish for something that didn't look too digital — the "timeless" essence meant a digital appearance would be perceived as belonging to the current time period — Deepend opted for simple HTML. The clean design created Conran's desired visual feel, while at the same time catering for the site's 300-odd pages of information.

Conran had never had all its products in one place before. Instead, they had always been separated and the company relied on people making connections between its services. The design team at Deepend decided to instil Conran's lifestyle and design philosophies into four distinct areas: Eat, Shop, Live and Us. That way, the different aspects of the brand could all be represented under the conran.com umbrella, but still hold identities independent enough for users to appreciate the difference.

It's all a far cry from the original Conran site. The company had initially approached Deepend to find a solution to its online shop problem — whether it should be a summary of all the offline shops, or whether it should be its own unique space — but ended up with a complete redesign. "The old site had grown organically which meant there was no structure to it, so it was difficult working out where things were within the site's architecture," says Nicky Gibson, a senior designer at Deepend. "The previous site had also taken the brand guidelines that worked very well in print and translated them in quite an obvious way. Even when we started dealing with Conran, the company wasn't used to seeing its brand online, and so had to get used to the medium."

As a result, Conran, like a lot of clients, was quite unaccustomed to dealing with new media and was somewhat entrenched in its old print

EAT SHOP LIVE US

THE
CONRAN
SHOP

EAT SHOP LIVE US

HOME

CONRAN SHOPS
ONLINE SHOPPING
SPECIAL OFFERS

| **HOMEOFFICE**

STATIONERY
STORAGE

MY ACCOUNT
SHOPPING BASKET
CUSTOMER INFORMATION

work
with style

Conran adds a unique style to
an efficient and versatile work
space - everything from a mouse
mat to a complete work station.

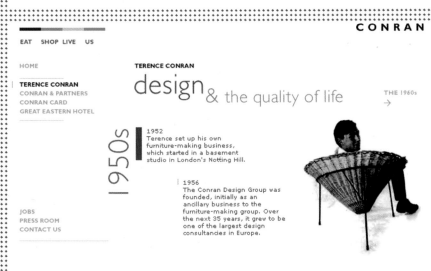

CONRAN

EAT SHOP LIVE US

HOME

TERENCE CONRAN
CONRAN & PARTNERS
CONRAN CARD
GREAT EASTERN HOTEL

TERENCE CONRAN

design & the quality of life

THE 1960s
→

1950s

| 1952
Terence set up his own
furniture-making business,
which started in a basement
studio in London's Notting Hill.

| 1956
The Conran Design Group was
founded, initially as an
ancillary business to the
furniture-making group. Over
the next 35 years, it grew to be
one of the largest design
consultancies in Europe.

JOBS
PRESS ROOM
CONTACT US

EAT SHOP LIVE US

CONRAN RESTAURANTS

**Text is as important to the brand as
design and experience. Conran made
sure that Deepend got the tone of the
site's copy just right.**

HOME

A-Z OF RESTAURANTS
INSPIRE ME
ONLINE BOOKING
PRIVATE DINING
CONRAN CARD
SPECIAL OFFERS

THE FOOD

Our chefs use only the very
best ingredients, often
seasonal, organic and grown
exclusively for us by small
artisan suppliers. Whether
you have a craving for fish
and chips or a passion for
Italian food - we have a
variety of restaurants to suit.

In which type of restaurant
would you like to eat?

Inspire me to eat

STYLE OF COOKING

| Japanese ⬍ |

SELECT →

JOBS

world. The company could only describe its look through brochures and magazine articles. "At the start, Conran didn't really know how to communicate its brand," says Jackie Lea, Deepend's account director on the project. "It wasn't until we started designing that Conran could see how to talk to us about it. It's quite common. Most clients say they want the picture bigger or the logo bigger because when they open up their brochure they've got a brilliant flat colour on one side and a massive image on the other. So that's what they think they want on their websites. It's quite a struggle to explain that you have more impact when you don't have to spend 20 minutes downloading the first page."

One of the biggest concerns for Conran was the tone of the site's copy. Criminally overlooked on a lot of projects, text shapes an online brand as much as design, and Conran recognized this from the off. Strictly observing the way Deepend's copywriters phrased things, the company was quite particular about using terms such as "shop" and "eat", rather than "e-commerce" and "dining".

"It often comes secondary to design, but the tone of the copy is just as important," says Jane Austin, a usability designer at Deepend. "Talking to someone in the wrong way can severely damage your brand, especially online, where it has a much stronger impact than on a billboard. Here, you have to make the effort to use it and it's an experience that stays with you. If you take the time to interact with it and it's not written correctly, it has a much worse effect than seeing something that passes you by. And with the Web, one bad experience is all people need never to come back again."

EAT   SHOP LIVE   US

HOME
_____

CONRAN SHOPS
ONLINE SHOPPING
SPECIAL OFFERS
_____

ONLINE DEPARTMENTS
_____

DRINKING AND SMOKING
GLASSWARE
KITCHEN ACCESSORIES
TABLETOP

_____

MY ACCOUNT
SHOPPING BASKET
CUSTOMER INFORMATION
_____

Deepend kept the Conran site clean and clear to incorporate the company's many business assets in one place for the first time.

THE
CONRAN
SHOP

KITCHEN ▊ drinking & smoking

| **1** | £37.00 | **02** | £60.00 | **03** | £29.95 | **04** | £12.95 |

Verve Wine
Bucket

MORE
INFO

ADD TO
BASKET

Wine Cooler

MORE
INFO

ADD TO
BASKET

Ice Bucket

MORE
INFO

ADD TO
BASKET

Ice Tongs

MORE
INFO

ADD TO
BASKET

MORE PRODUCTS →

www.guardian.co.uk

CLIENT: Guardian Unlimited
DESIGNED BY: In-house
DEVELOPMENT TIME: 8 months
SIZE OF PROJECT TEAM: 12 people
TECHNOLOGY USED: DDX story server, Fireworks, Flash, HTML, Photoshop and Quicktime
CONTACT: www.guardian.co.uk

CONSISTENCY, CONSISTENCY, CONSISTENCY. DELIVERING A UNIFORM BRAND ACROSS THE WHOLE NETWORK WAS GUARDIAN UNLIMITED'S CENTRAL CONCERN

The Guardian Unlimited network is that rarest of breeds: an Internet brand that's been there since the beginning. Launched at a time when having a traditional media brand-name association was a disadvantage, the Unlimited sites rolled out as a series of single brands — newsunlimited, football-unlimited, filmunlimited — left to fight their own market and define their own audiences. It has learnt over time that ties with the Guardian newspaper itself are more powerful, and a rebranding exercise in late 2000 unified the sites under the Guardian Unlimited (GU) umbrella.

The Guardian and GU try and challenge the status quo. Both serve as a place to find alternative opinions and, as The Editor, The Guardian's Friday supplement, summarizes the week's news from the viewpoint of other newspapers, so too does the Unlimited network. "When the Web first started, people were desperate to keep their audiences, but we've always provided links to other sites so we can extend the story," says Chris Moisan, GU's head of channels. "It provides more of a service that way, and good branding has got to be a service. You have to deliver something of value to your users."

The two clearly have their differences, though. "When the Web came along, a lot of people predicted the death of newspapers, but it's actually a really different media offering," says Chris. "People consume digital content very differently to newspaper content. Newspaper readership has become a leisure activity because people now get their news from a million other sources, including the Web. GU serves a different need: it supplies the breaking news, which the paper can't do, and the full story. A newspaper is constrained to a set number of pages and a specific type of content. Covering the terrorist attacks on America on 11 September 2001, for example, The Guardian provided expert opinion and analysis. The GU, however,

The Brody Blocks, Guardian Unlimited's top-level navigation boxes, help give the network a solid consistency, both visually and in terms of weighting editorial content.

Guardian Unlimited

THE · WRAP

Guardian Unlimited FreshDelivery

The UK's most popular newspaper website

Log in

Go to: [Guardian Unlimited home ▼] [Go]

travel

Home | Countries | Cities | Activities | Weekenders | Late offers | Talk
Links | Netjetters | News | Travel light | Ask a traveller | Marketplace | Help

Attack on Afghanistan Travel advice following the strikes

Board room Our pick of the best resorts for snowboarders this winter

Fantasy football Get in the mood for 2002 with our World Cup venue guide

Tuesday October 9 2001

Search

 [Go]

About this site ◢

Readers' offers ◢

Terrorism's legacy: special report

Audio cities guide ◢

UK interactive guide ◢

Guide to the World Cup 2002 venues

Can you take the bliss?
Bali's charms have long been the preserve of the wealthy, but that may be changing. We sent two writers - one with £2,500, the other £500 - to see if you still need a pot of cash to enjoy the Indonesian archipelago's top attraction
More on Indonesia

Dreaming of the right Christmas?
Dee O'Connell seeks out some alternatives to festive fatigue
Feliz Navidad! Christmas in Madrid

Where everything stops for tea
Some of the best tea rooms in Britain
Food and drink: special report

People consume digital content very differently to newspaper content. The Guardian Unlimited network can create interactive guides that just aren't possible offline.

Guardian Unlimited

THE CITY THE WHOLE CITY NOTHING BUT THE CITY. VOLVO S40 & V40

Go to: [Guardian Unlimited home ▲▼] [Go]

travel Countries

Home | Countries | Cities | Activities | Weekenders | Late offers | Talk
Links | Netjetters | News | Travel light | Ask a traveller | Marketplace | Help

Indonesia
Two sides of Bali

Can you take the bliss?

It's the Far East's most magical island, but Bali's charms have long been the preserve of the wealthy - Sting and the Beckhams included. Yet that seems to be changing. We sent two writers there - one with £2,500 to spend, the other £500 - to see if you still need a pot of cash to enjoy the Indonesian archipelago's top attraction. Jill Hartley enjoyed the posh experience, while Burhan Wazir's time there was cheap but still cheerful

Sunday October 7, 2001
The Observer

Search

[   ] [Go]

The leading website for Spanish wines

Before you decide whether you can take a 16-hour flight (including a stop in Singapore), an eight-hour time change and a hefty clout at your credit card to stay in Bali's five-star finest resorts, ask yourself: Am I a sensual being?

was able to create interactive guides that showed the event, the location and the geographical and economic situation in Afghanistan. The structure of the Internet enables us to expand the story and let people follow it through to as many different areas as they want."

Developing the story further while keeping the same philosophy as the paper helped GU exploit the Internet's facilities, while remaining true to its offline ethics. Its main concern, though, was creating a uniform brand across the whole network.

"Consistency is essential," explains Chris. "Each site is individually accessible and has its own personality and navigation, but there are a lot of similarities in terms of movement and functionality." The main strand that holds all the sites together is GU's common grid functionality. Each site has a series of rectangular areas below its top-level navigation. These are known as the Brody Blocks — the

site was originally designed by Neville Brody — and are a prime area where editorial can promote its latest features and specials. "The blocks are replicated throughout the entire network, so, if you want the most significant stories, you always know where to look," says Chris. "The grid system helps give the sites a solid consistency, both visually and in terms of weighting editorial content."

And GU knows how important consistency is to its users. When the network first launched, its football talkboards were strong and fitted in well with the rest of the footballunlimited site. One redesign later, and several founders of the community had left to set up their own talk group. To them, the talkboard was no longer consistent with the way the site worked. "With any change you're going to upset people, but our problem was that we didn't make it compatible with the rest of the site," says Chris. "You have to make it consistent."

www.guinnessstorehouse.com

CLIENT: Guinness
DESIGNED BY: Imagination
DEVELOPMENT TIME: 6 months
SIZE OF PROJECT TEAM: 5 people
TECHNOLOGY USED: After Effects, Flash, Freehand, HTML, Illustrator, Photoshop and Streamline
CONTACT: www.imagination.co.uk

"If people are asking questions all the time, it encourages them to go and find out the answers for themselves. It's about getting people involved with the brand, rather than serving them information on a plate (or in a glass)"

CREATING·A·TEASER·FOR·THE·GUINNESS·STOREHOUSE
IN·DUBLIN,·IMAGINATION·MADE·USERS·INTERACT·WITH
THE·BRAND·TO·WHET·THEIR·APPETITE·FOR·MORE

The Guinness Storehouse site gives just enough
information away to get people interested and
enable them to understand what it's all about before
they go.

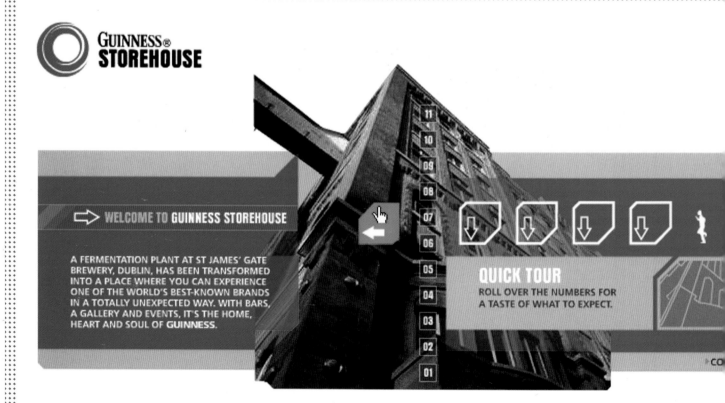

GUINNESS®
STOREHOUSE

⇨ **WELCOME TO GUINNESS STOREHOUSE**

A FERMENTATION PLANT AT ST JAMES' GATE
BREWERY, DUBLIN, HAS BEEN TRANSFORMED
INTO A PLACE WHERE YOU CAN EXPERIENCE
ONE OF THE WORLD'S BEST-KNOWN BRANDS
IN A TOTALLY UNEXPECTED WAY. WITH BARS,
A GALLERY AND EVENTS, IT'S THE HOME,
HEART AND SOUL OF **GUINNESS**.

QUICK TOUR
ROLL OVER THE NUMBERS FOR
A TASTE OF WHAT TO EXPECT.

11
10
09
08
07
06
05
04
03
02
01

▸ **TERMS & CONDITIONS**
▸ **PRIVACY POLICY**

WHAT HAPPENS IF YOU COMBINE LUCK, AMBITION AND SHEER DETERMINATION? PICK A CHAPTER IN THE **ARTHUR GUINNESS** STORY AND WATCH THE PICTURE COMPLETE BEFORE YOUR EYES.

AT THE TOP OF THE **GUINNESS STOREHOUSE**, IT FEELS LIKE THE TOP OF THE WORLD. HERE YOU'LL FIND **GRAVITY**, A BAR WHERE YOU CAN ENJOY A FREE PINT OF **GUINNESS** AND TAKE IN ONE OF THE BEST VIEWS OVER DUBLIN. PERFECT. JUST MOVE YOUR CURSOR TO THE LEFT OR RIGHT TO SEE HOW SPECTACULAR IT IS.

Guinness is well and truly entrenched in perceptions of Irish culture. Sinking a few pints of the black stuff is now an essential part of any trip to Dublin — as is a trip to the new Guinness Storehouse, a brand centre that serves as "the ultimate expression of the character of Guinness".

When it came to transferring the Storehouse experience in the Irish capital of Dublin to the Web, London-based Imagination had one big advantage. It had already designed and built the actual Storehouse itself. Imagination was able to work closely with the other disciplines within its company to recreate this brand centre online — from understanding what people would be experiencing instore to animating the vortex, the Storehouse logo that represents the circular motion of the journey through the building.

The Guinness Storehouse site is about selling the experience; tempting people to make the journey to Dublin and find out the rest of the story for themselves. "Guinness wanted to create a glimpse of what people could expect to find; just enough to get them interested and enable them to understand

what it's all about before
they go," says David
Chamberlain, a senior designer
at Imagination. "We thought
about it in the same way that
people make trailers for the
cinema — show the best bits
and whet people's appetites,
so that when they go to the
Storehouse they can pick up
on the rest of the story.
That's how we wanted to
treat this site."

Most visitors to the site know
little about the Storehouse
other than the fact it's a
new offering from Guinness.
The introduction places the
Storehouse's location and
physical appearance, but the
"Explore" section is the area
of the site that really
communicates what the store
is all about. Using Flash
to create an interactive
experience of motion graphics
and sound, Imagination sought
to make the online Guinness
Storehouse as close to the
Dublin original as possible.
The "Explore" section is
built like the Storehouse,
a fluid journey across seven
floors of interactive
exhibitions that visitors can
dip in and out of as they
wish. The content structure
reflects the pint-glass-

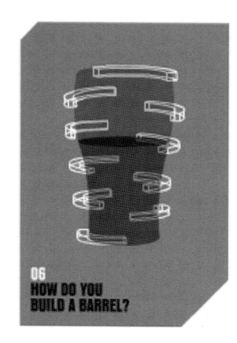

06
HOW DO YOU
BUILD A BARREL?

HOW DO YOU
BUILD A BARREL?

WHAT'S IT LIKE TO BE WORKING IN INTE
AND SHEER STRENGTH TO BUILD A GU
THINK YOU COULD DO IT? WHY NOT GI

▸ TERMS & CONDITIONS
▸ PRIVACY POLICY

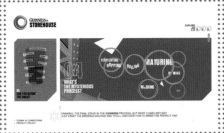

EXPLORE

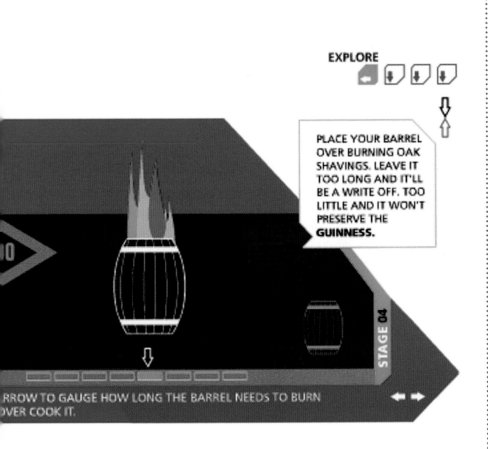

PLACE YOUR BARREL OVER BURNING OAK SHAVINGS. LEAVE IT TOO LONG AND IT'LL BE A WRITE OFF. TOO LITTLE AND IT WON'T PRESERVE THE **GUINNESS.**

STAGE 04

RROW TO GAUGE HOW LONG THE BARREL NEEDS TO BURN
OVER COOK IT.

EAT AND NOISE, USING YOUR SKILL
BARREL. IT'S NOT A JOB FOR THE FAINT-HEARTED.
GO?

The essence of Imagination's Guinness Storehouse experience is interaction with the brand – from presentations on Guinness's history and role today, to exploring cooperage and what goes into a pint of Ireland's favourite stout.

shaped atrium of the Storehouse and even the sounds on the site are taken from the building itself.

"We wanted to create a way of navigating through the site that reflected the way people used the Storehouse," says David. "The 'Ingredients' area in the building has a waterfall, so we've taken that metaphor and used what goes into making a pint of Guinness for each waterfall strand. It's very top-level information, as people will find out more when they make the trip, but the way they find out this information reflects the Storehouse experience."

Users work their way through presentations on Guinness's history, brewing process, cooperage, role in Irish life and advertising. The core of Imagination's Guinness Storehouse experience is getting the user to interact with the brand. Each presentation requires some sort of interaction from the

user — the Arthur Guinness exhibition has seven storeys that build up into a shape as each one is read, while the "Cooperage" section requires users to click and drag the barrels into shape. Making people discover things for themselves gives them a much better feeling of what the Guinness Storehouse brand is all about.

Imagination enhances this by making many of the presentations question-based. What's the mysterious process? What's the missing link? Users are pushed into wanting to find out. "We always pose a question and then provide an answer at the end of the user's interaction," says Damien Ferrar, head of multimedia at Imagination. "If people are asking questions all the time, it encourages them to go and find out the answers for themselves. It's about getting people involved with the brand, rather than serving them information on a plate (or in a glass)."

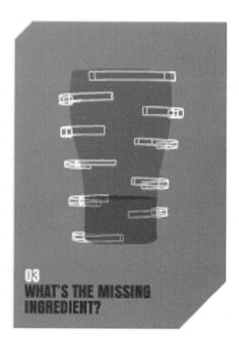

03
WHAT'S THE MISSING INGREDIENT?

▸ TERMS & CONDITIONS
▸ PRIVACY POLICY

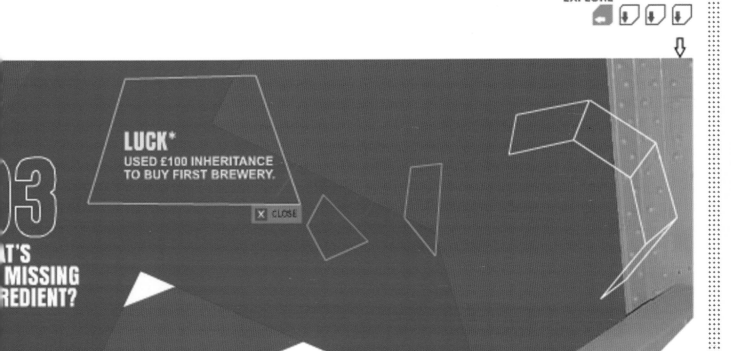

LUCK*
USED £100 INHERITANCE
TO BUY FIRST BREWERY.

X CLOSE

03

AT'S
MISSING
REDIENT?

APPENS IF YOU COMBINE LUCK, AMBITION AND SHEER DETERMINATION?
CHAPTER IN THE **ARTHUR GUINNESS** STORY AND WATCH THE PICTURE
ETE BEFORE YOUR EYES.

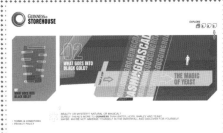

www.habitat.net

CLIENT: Habitat

DESIGNED BY: Digit

DEVELOPMENT TIME: 6 months

SIZE OF PROJECT TEAM: 10 people

TECHNOLOGY USED: Flash, Java and XML

CONTACT: www.digit1.com

"Every time the desktop icon delivers a new piece of design inspiration, it presents some dialogue that just makes people think about their living environment. After all, that's what Habitat the brand is all about"

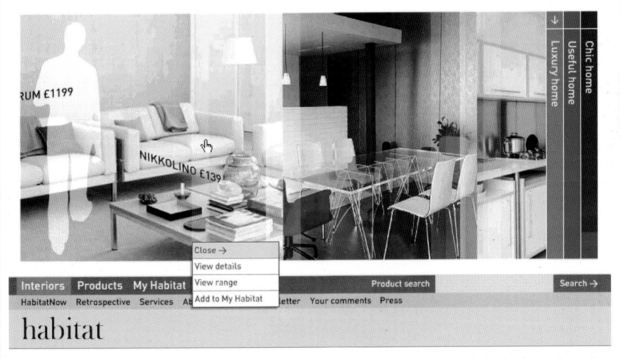

HABITAT■INSPIRES■ITS■CUSTOMERS.■DIGIT
MADE■SURE■ITS■WEBSITE■CARRIED■ON■THAT
TASK■AND■PROVIDED■A■SERVICE■TO■BOOT

Interiors

Feel free to browse around our Habitat homes.
Move through our many different room sets,
and click for details on our featured products.

Interiors   Products   My Habitat   Product search

HabitatNow   Retrospective   Services   About our stores   Newsletter   Your comments   Press

habitat

Good afternoon, welcom

Digit used a lot of imagery to replicate the Habitat catalogue online. The "Interiors" section enables users to stroll through room sets, as if they were in the store.

Skip intro →

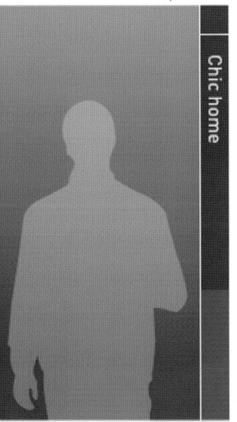

Chic home

Search →

.habitat.net

One of the most important aspects of online branding is making sure your message is consistent with offline campaigns and communication. Habitat's site wasn't, so London-based Digit set about making sure it didn't stay that way for long. "Habitat's pan-European site really needed to work harder for the brand," says Rob Cooke, Digit's strategic director. "It wasn't in tandem with what Habitat was trying to achieve in the store, and there was very little synergy with the one thing that everyone knows about Habitat — its catalogue."

The Habitat catalogue is a seminal tome that has traditionally been the voice of the company — it determines the company's look and feel, which change on a seasonal basis. Habitat has always taken the view that if it defines itself today, then it's going to be out of date tomorrow. Its brand guidelines are as fluid as possible and, as a result, the company has survived and adapted since the 1950s.

"The catalogue is a way of providing people with inspiration, and we've tried to reflect that in the way we've designed the site," says Rob. "A lot of people don't like to be told what's trendy, but they do like to discover what's in and what's out. The catalogue is divided into various sections and room-sets — fusions of different products put together to give people ideas. The site works in the same way."

The essence of Habitat is its furnishing products, and the site has been split into three main areas for people to find what they're looking for: "Interiors", "Products" and the "MyHabitat" sections. For the "At Home" section, Digit decided to reflect the experience customers have when they visit Habitat stores. Users wander through the section, browsing for inspiration rather than being directed anywhere specific. Rolling over a product reveals colour and fabric availability, and gives you the choice of printing the image, sending it to a friend or even emailing your local store to see if they've got it in stock. It all adds up to what Digit hopes is a very tactile experience.

"Giving Habitat's products an extra dimension helped create a sense of people living within this particular space," says

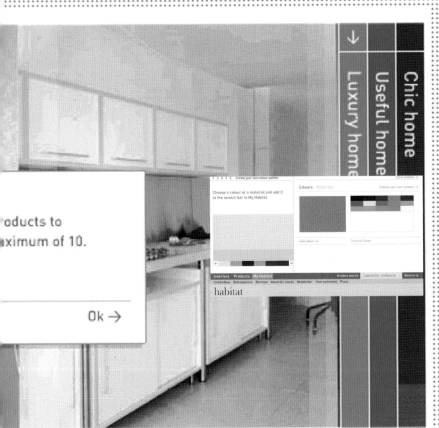

"MyHabitat" is a mood board that acts as a shopping basket for users to drag in their chosen products and play with background, size, colour and texture.

Toby Evetts, Digit's director of content. "Habitat is a very human brand. It's a brand that lives in people's lives, so this was a key point in the way in which this was approached. A lot of design companies approach online branding as a way of transferring the look, but it's the way of translating what the brand stands for emotionally that's really important."

The second area of navigation, the "Products" section, is for customers wanting to carry out more linear searches and the clearest indicator that Habitat is a pan-European site. Rather than just listing the products, Digit divided the home into various rooms, stocking each in the knowledge that people in Spain use their living rooms very differently to people in the UK and Germany. In all, there are about 14 different ways of getting to any one product.

The final navigation area, "MyHabitat", acts as a shopping basket where you can drag in images of your chosen products and play with the background, size, colour and texture. It's another way of

virtually bringing Habitat into people's homes. "'MyHabitat' is a mood board," says Brad Smith, a senior designer at Digit. "It enables you to explore swatches and product colours. It's a digital take on the experience of decorating."

Every aspect of design on the Habitat site, every animation and way of navigating, enforces Habitat's overall proposition of enriching people's lives; that Habitat has a suggestion for lighting, for cooking, for how you structure your kitchen and your dining room. Having established this so successfully online, Digit looked to continue the site's dialogue with the customers with occasional mailouts. The design agency came up with a little push engine, a downloadable desktop icon, that delivers a simple piece of design inspiration on a weekly basis — from inside-out flower arranging to coral farming. "Every time the icon delivers a new titbit of info, it presents some dialogue that just makes people think about their living environment," says Rob. "After all, that's what Habitat the brand is all about."

Interiors Products My Ha

HabitatNow Retrospective Service

habitat

Close details→

Clara

Armchair
Polyurethane foam-covered
frame. Cover 70 % wool, 20 %
polyamide, 10 % cashmere.
Powder coated tubular metal legs.
Metal and plastic castors. Height
adjustable. Swivel mechanism and
adjustable tilter.

Seat height: 47 to 54 cm.
W. 64 H. 90 cm.

1 / 2 →

Options →

Product search   Search →

ut our stores   Newsletter   Your comments   Press

www.eu.levi.com

CLIENT: Levi's
DESIGNED BY: Good Technology
DEVELOPMENT TIME: 4 ½ months
SIZE OF TEAM: 8 people
TECHNOLOGY USED: BlueMartini, Flash, Photoshop and Quicktime
CONTACT: www.goodtechnology.com

"Brands make mistakes when they treat the Web as just another marketing-communications tool and don't think of what value it can add to consumers as a medium"

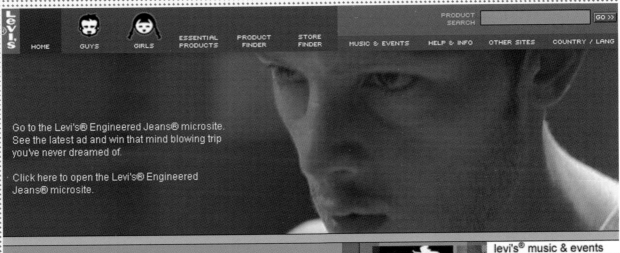

GOOD•TECHNOLOGY•REDESIGNED•THE•LEVI'S•EUROPE•SITE•TO
REPLICATE•THE•COMPANY'S•FLAGSHIP•STORES•AND•GIVE•ITS
INTERNET-PROFICIENT•AUDIENCE•WHAT•THEY•WANTED•

make levi.com >> fit you

1.

select >> your language
choisissez >> votre langue
wähle >> deine Sprache

[English ▼]

2.

select country for >>
product info >>
events >>
links to buying Levi's® products

[United Kingdom ▼]

3.

ready >>

go >>

Availability of products varies and not all products shown may be available in your selected country
© 2002, N.V. Levi Strauss & Co Europe S.A., all rights reserved.
N.V. Levi Strauss & Co Europe S.A., Trade Registry : RCB/HRB 453.557, VAT: BE 424.656.991

[PRIVACY >> STATEMENT] [TERMS >> CONDITIONS]

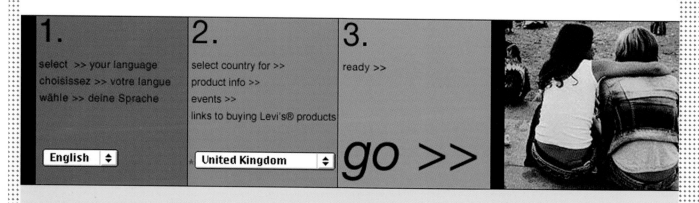

LEVI'S® ENGINEERED
JEANS®

Loose fit with twisted seams.
click product for more info

40201

Yves Saint Laurent once said that he has only one regret: that he didn't invent jeans. The fashion guru was beaten to it by a good hundred years. Levi Strauss created the first tough-working denims in 1853, and the brand has become a hallmark for generations of young people ever since.

"The Levi's brand is iconic; it symbolizes all the great things about being young," says Anne Bonew, digital marketing manager of Levi Strauss Europe. "It's a brand that equips young people to change their world."

Levi's appeal to the young breaks through national barriers — the company has the same image in the UK as it does in Italy. "Levi's portrays itself very consistently across Europe," says Xanthe Arvanitakis, client services director at Good Technology. "Europeans all see the same adverts, the same brand. The flagship store in Spain will look the same as it does in London. You don't really need to alter youth brands for the local market because you're talking to a certain proportion of people who all want to be the same across Europe."

It was these flagship stores that Good Technology aimed to replicate in developing the Levi's Europe site. "Consistency is the driver of our online presence: the overall site design is inspired by our physical store design," says Anne. "The site has a specific role in the communication mix; it has to reinforce other brand messages and to prompt consumers to visit the stores. Therefore, all visual elements of the site are built to provide an integrated brand experience to consumers: when a window display changes in a store, the homepage will change as well."

The Levi's Europe site is designed to reflect the company's flagship stores in attitude and appearance. The site also changes in keeping with the storefront displays.

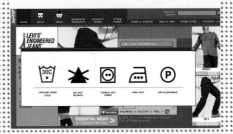

HOME   GUYS   GIRLS   ESSENTIAL PRODUCTS   PRODUCT FINDER   STORE FINDER   MUSIC & EVENTS

buy in-store >>

buy online >>

find a Levi's® store >> near you >> enter a city >> and any other info you know >> for better results

buy online >> your Levi's® products >> delivered to you

STREET ADDRESS

CITY

*

POST CODE

COUNTRY

United Kingdom

MANDATORY

SEARCH >>

ZOOVILLAGE.COM

Your local streetwear store. Open 24 hrs.

shotgun

<< Graphic spray finish on long sleeve raglan tee
43529
click product for more info

RED TAB®
Contrast Denim

nternational >>

de >> Levi's® stores

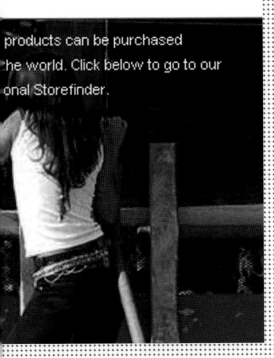

products can be purchased
he world. Click below to go to our
onal Storefinder.

Levi's is well known for its television adverts, but,
in the case of its website, Good Technology
believed that the best offering the site could make
was to give the consumer a feel for the product
before they even enter the store.

Before Good Technology
stepped in, the site had
been pretty much a marketing
brochure. It was the agency's
job to turn it into a
consumer-centric site and
provide services to users
that were more a part of the
shopping experience. It's a
shift that Xanthe thinks was
vital to the Levi's online
presence. "Brands make
mistakes when they treat the
Web as just another marketing-
communications tool and don't
think of what value it can
add to consumers as a
medium," she says. "Levi's
will hold its hands up and
say it was making that
mistake with its audience.
Youths are heavy Internet
users, and yet Levi's was
effectively giving them an
online PR brochure. They
expected to find the product,
get a feel for the product
and get a feel for the brand
before going out to the
shops."

The Levi's audience can now
browse for products online,
connect with their local
stores and keep up to date
with seasonal fashion lines.
Levi's markets itself on a
cycle — as part of each new
season, the company launches
a new above-the-line campaign
— so Good Technology is able
to regularly update the site
with new ideas, new events
and new products. The
redesign now lives beyond
the creative campaigns and
gives an online audience
what it wants from a Levi's
website. "Levi's makes
beautiful advertising films
for television but in its
website's case, the best
offering Levi's can make
is to give the consumer a
really interesting branded
experience that they can
scroll through before going
into the store," says Xanthe.
"Traditional brands have
years of offline investment
behind them, but what makes
good online branding is when
you marry what's right for
the company with what's right
for the medium."

SOUND ON/OFF ☐

Exit to levi.com (Europe)

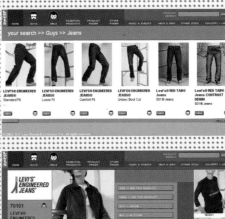

www.mercedes-benz.co.uk

CLIENT: Mercedes-Benz

DESIGNED BY: Rufus Leonard

DEVELOPMENT TIME: 4 months

SIZE OF PROJECT TEAM: 12 people

TECHNOLOGY USED: HTML, DHTML, Flash and Photoshop

CONTACT: www.rufusleonard.com

"Mercedes's new objective was to get every person in the UK to aspire to own a Mercedes. It was a populist message, and one that was completely different from the way the brand was perceived when we first started working with it"

Mercedes-Benz

Cars Home | Terms | Go Global

>> Go to

| MODEL RANGE » | RETAIL NETWORK | SHOWROOM | USED CARS | FINANCIAL SERVICES | AFTERCARE | CONTACT US |

SL-Class

▸ OVERVIEW
▸ FEATURES
COMPARE
▸ SL 500
▸ SL 55 AMG
GALLERY
OWNERSHIP
PRICE LIST
PERSONAL COLLECTION

The SL 500
a dynamic beauty ▸

The SL 55 AMG
an exhilarating performer ▸

The new SL-Class.
The ultimate sports car.

RUFUS·LEONARD'S·NEW·SITE·FOR·MERCEDES-BENZ·NOT
ONLY·REPOSITIONS·THE·COMPANY·FOR·DIFFERENT
MARKETS·BUT·ENABLES·ITS·USERS·TO·MAINTAIN·A
DIRECT·RELATIONSHIP·WITH·THE·BRAND

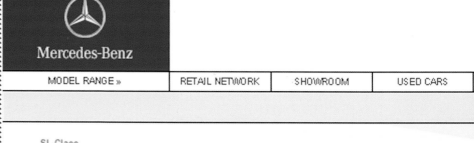

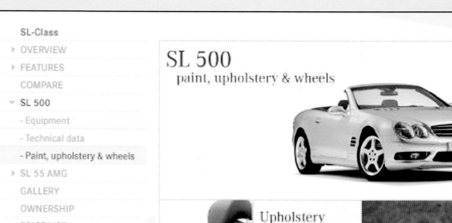

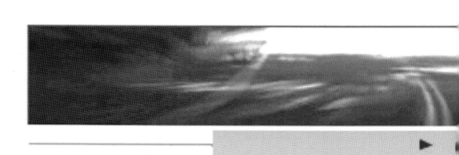

Mercedes-Benz's traditional market, cars, is about building
a relationship between the brand and the consumer.

Cars Home | Terms | Go Global

>> Go to ⬍

| SERVICES | AFTERCARE | CONTACT US |

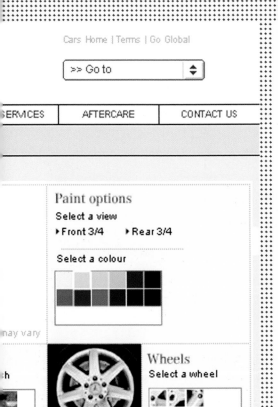

Paint options

Select a view
▸ Front 3/4   ▸ Rear 3/4

Select a colour

may vary

Wheels
Select a wheel

ih

The launch of Mercedes-Benz's "For Whoever You Are" campaign marked the culmination in the German car manufacturer's gradual rebranding process. Mercedes had been working with London agency Rufus Leonard for two years and it was this new campaign, combined with the company's subsequent desire to develop the UK site's structure as a more accurate reflection of the way its business was developing, that instigated Rufus Leonard's redesign of mercedes-benz.co.uk.

"Mercedes-Benz's new objective was to get every person in the UK to aspire to own a Mercedes," says Andrew Pinkess, Rufus Leonard's strategy director. "It was a populist message, and one that was completely different from the way the brand was perceived when we first started working with it. Making the website reflect this has had to be done in quite a sensitive way because one of the things that people have traditionally liked about Mercedes is its exclusiveness, that it's not a brand for everyone. We had to design the site in a way that welcomed new customers, but still made the traditional fat-cat clients feel that they continued to have a home with Mercedes-Benz."

Previously rolled into one large area, the site is now split into distinct sections — cars, vans and trucks — that recognize the needs of Mercedes's very different audiences and help clarify the equally different approaches Mercedes is making to each market. Nadia Turan,

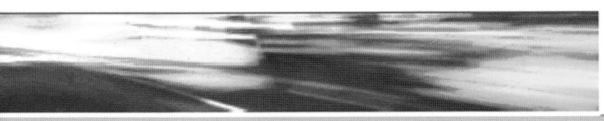

▶ Vans   ▶ Trucks

a lead designer at Rufus Leonard, explains: "Mercedes's positioning in the vans and trucks market is very different to its positioning in the car market. Vans and trucks are all about hardcore business — they want to know the weight, volume, reliability, economy and resale value. The car market, however, is much more about building a relationship and creating an environment that consumers feel comfortable with."

Audience attitude doesn't change just between markets, though. It can change between models. An A-Class driver is clearly going to have a different profile from the guy who slips behind the wheel of a Z3. "We're working on making that more prevalent in the design, look and feel of the environment," says Andrew. "You need to be confident about the brand DNA that runs throughout the site, but you can't be afraid of talking to an audience directly when you know what that audience profile is. Over the last couple of years Mercedes-Benz equalled an obsession with engineering and product quality, the badge was a symbol for total reliability and engineering excellence. It still is, but now the badge means something

MODEL RANGE »

| RETAIL NETWORK | SHOWROOM | US |
| Hatchbacks | Saloons | Estates |

For whoever y

Cars Home | Terms | Go Global

>> Go to

FINANCIAL SERVICES	AFTERCARE	CONTACT US
Coupés	MPV	Off-Roader	AMG

u are

The two new
A-Classes

Find out more ▶▶

Personal **Collection**
Stuttgart ▶

World of Mercedes-Benz ▶

The new
C-Class Estate ▶

Repositioning itself to target audiences in the vans and trucks sector meant that other areas of the site were all about hardcore business – weight, volume and reliability.

Mercedes-Benz

>> Go To

| DEALERS | USED VANS | FINANCIAL SERVICES | AFTER SALES | NEWS | CONTACT US |

VAN RANGE ▸

Sprinter CDI home
▸ Sprinter CDI range
▸ PERFORMANCE
▸ PRACTICALITY
▸ ECONOMY
▸ COMFORT
▸ OPTIONAL EXTRAS
▸ SAFETY
▸ PAINT AND UPHOLSTERY
▸ ENVIRONMENT
▸ GALLERY
▸ Vans home

Sprinter
Powerful yet economical

The Mercedes-Benz Sprinter is the UK's leading light commercial vehicle. Available in three types: Panel Van, Chassis Cab and the Travelliner, the Sprinter combines reliability with great versatility. The Sprinter: A cost effective addition to your business.

| Home | Real Life Stories | The Facts | Take a Test Drive | Brochure Request | Offers |

Take a Vito, and choose 1 of these 3:
– 3 years free servicing
– Accessory package
– Operating lease

VITO

See for yourself. Take a test drive ▶

"I drive a Vito"
Get a taste for life with a Vito through our real life stories. Vito owners talk about their vans.

Just the f
Need to know ho
can fit in a Vito?
Get straight to th

Vito. Take one to feel better about your business.

more than that. It's a lifestyle choice."

In addition to Mercedes's brand repositioning, the site was also due for a structural overhaul. When it was first developed, "direct purchasing" was a powerful buzzword. Experience, however, proved that few people were prepared to actually buy cars over the Web. They would rather use a car site to qualify their purchase and be better informed when they visit the car dealers. Mercedes has now become an advice-giver; a brand that helps its customers when they step onto the forecourt. "The new site is enabling Mercedes to communicate more effectively with its customers and, in doing so, establish a better relationship with them," says Andrew. "The dynamics have changed. In the past, cars would be sold from the showroom by the dealer and Mercedes wouldn't even know who its customers were." The new site has enabled Mercedes's customers to maintain a relationship directly with the brand throughout their model's life-cycle.

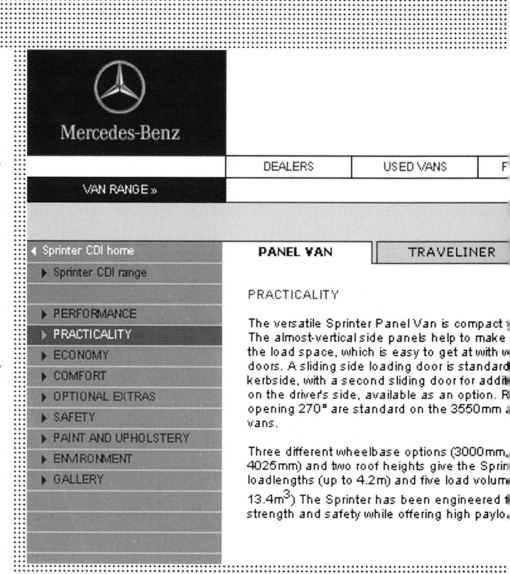

>> Go To ⬍

SERVICES | AFTER SALES | NEWS | CONTACT US

CHASSIS CAB

us.
of all
ing

bility
s
mm

, and

ities.

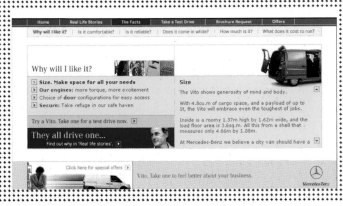

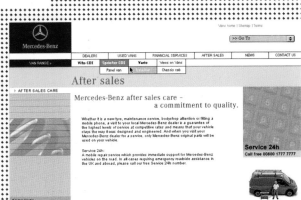

www.m-three.com

CLIENT: Millennium Three

DESIGNED BY: Paris France

DEVELOPMENT TIME: 3 ½ months

SIZE OF PROJECT TEAM: 6 people

TECHNOLOGY USED: Flash, i-Movie, Quicktime, Photoshop, Sound Edit 16 and XML

CONTACT: www.paris-france.com

"Demonstrating that the riders
essentially run the company is the
key to the brand's integrity.
Individuals will come and go, but M3
will always be the brand that's
built by riders for riders"

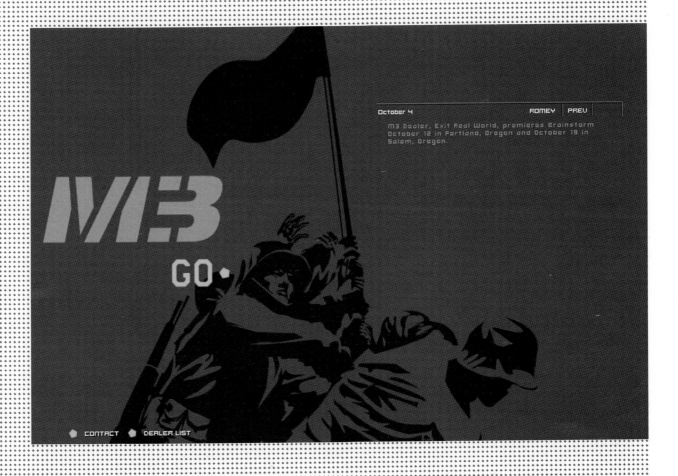

BY■ALIENATING■OUTSIDERS■AND■EMPHASIZING■THE
ROLE■PROFESSIONAL■RIDERS■PLAY,■PARIS■FRANCE
HAS■ENHANCED■M3'S■SNOWBOARDING■INTEGRITY

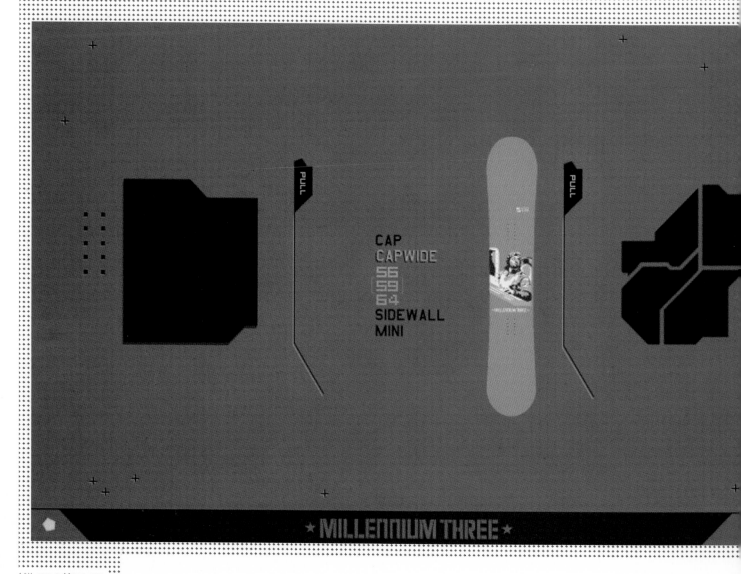

CAP
CAPWIDE
56
59
64
SIDEWALL
MINI

PULL

PULL

★ MILLENNIUM THREE ★

The opening page of M3's site is deliberately constructed to alienate non-boarders. Only those involved in the sport would know the numbers stand for board lengths.

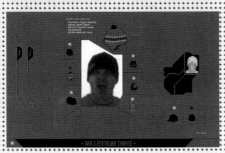

The seeds of Millennium Three (M3) were sown by a group of disillusioned professional snowboarders at Mount Hood, Oregon. Today, Blaise Rosenthal and the rest of the team of professional riders work on designing the boards, board graphics, brand advertising, catalogues and graphic design. Moreover, they are involved with the website itself. While having professionals ride the same boards as the average rider isn't unusual, having them so deeply involved in all areas of the company is. And it's a message M3 is keen to get across.

"Demonstrating that the riders essentially run the company is the key to the brand's integrity," says Doug Lowell, creative director at Portland-based Paris France and, alongside the agency's other creative director, Jeff Faulkner, the brains behind the M3 site. "Snowboarders are looking for a brand that stands for the idealism of their own dedication to snowboarding; a brand that isn't just a businessman hiding behind a hired rider. M3 is that brand. The riders are the originators of the brand, the living embodiment of the brand and they'll always be the future of the brand. Individuals will come and go, but M3 will always be the brand that's built by riders for riders."

Anyone who owns an M3 board can register on the site under the board they ride, right next to Blaise Rosenthal, Mikey LeBlanc and the other pro riders. A column from the team's manager gives the audience a behind-the-scenes look at the team's daily life, while Quicktime movies offer an extra insight into the riders' existences. By doing this, Paris France is inviting in the audience and involving them more with the team and with the brand.

The 2001 site's primary purpose was to integrate the stories of the riders and the boards and bring the two into balance, using the riders to introduce this year's line of boards in copy, audio and video. Since the M3 site isn't an e-commerce one, the ultimate objective is to get people to their local board shop to see the boards. "This is the third site we've done now and every year some aims stay the same and some change," says Doug. "In the past, the focus has been purely on the team riders. This year, because we'd already shown that the riders weren't just a bunch of shills, we were able to strike more of a balance

VIDEO

◆ RAILSLIDE

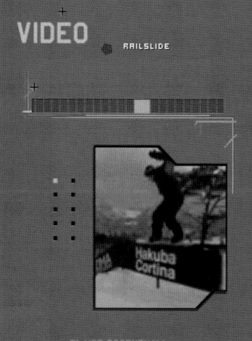

BLAISE ROSENTHALL

IMG
V ● ● H

BLAISE
ROSENTHAL

AGE 28

BOARD CAP, 57

LOCATION Truckee, CA

The worst thing that happened last year? I hurt my ankle, that sucked. The worst thing that ever happens to me is I just stress myself out worrying about filming or getting stuff done, I guess. I did that last year for sure just because the snow sucked so bad. I stressed out, that's probably the worst thing. I'm a professional snowboarder living in the wealthiest country in the world, I eat every day, I have a house with a bed in it. Nothing really bad ever actually happens to me, so it's all relative. There are people that are trying to

DIG THEIR FUCKING BREAKFAST

out of the ground right now, and I'm worrying about not getting my Cab 5 for my video parts. Kinda stupid.

★ MILLENNIUM THREE ★

VIDEO ◆ FRONTSIDE 810 TO FRONTSIDE BOARDSLIDE ◆ SWITCH BACKSIDE 180

MIKEY LEBLANC

IMG
V ● ● H

AGE 21

BOARD MAGNAFLI 88

LOCATION Gilman VT

I met a few people in the beginning—they were among those first few snowboarders I knew—and those kids that were like, "What do you want to do with that?" And they'd always nod me and for a year they'd be like "You want to be a pro snowboarder," and I was like "No I can't," even though in the back of my head I totally did. And they would always say,

**WELL IF YOU WANNA BE IT,
YOU JUST GOTTA BE IT.**

And then having one night my frame who's been raging the same thing, his home was Ball, he was like "You want to be a pro snowboarder, don't you, Mikey?" And I'm like, "No," and he's like "You totally do, I know you do. Why don't you just do it?" And it kinda hit home real hard. So it just made me do it.

MIKEY LEBLANC

★ MILLENNIUM THREE ★

VIDEO ◆ FRONTSIDE 360 OFF CLIFF ◆ CEMENT BOARDSLIDE

SCOTTY WITTLAKE

IMG
V ● ● H

AGE 22

BOARD MAGNAFLI 58

LOCATION Truckee CA

Scotty single-handedly has gotten on America's Most Wanted. Scotty has gotten a DUI, been banned from Southwest Airlines, and has probably been drinking about four thousand bottles of beer in the last two weeks.

Scotty got on a plane to go to Portland from Reno on Southwest and started talking about how he thought the plane was gonna blow up until one of the passengers decided they wanted to fight him and it ended up that Scotty got arrested, spent some time in airport jail, and got banned from Southwest for life.

So now anytime Scotty wants to fly anywhere like Portland or southern California or Salt Lake City he has to be routed through the Houston Texas or southern Arizona or somewhere.

THATS SCOTTY.

SCOTTY WITTLAKE

★ MILLENNIUM THREE ★

M3 is run by professional snowboarders. Demonstrating that the riders essentially run the company is key to the brand's integrity.

between the riders and their boards."

Either way, the focus is totally on snowboarding. Whereas a lot of websites try to appeal to a variety of users, the M3 site is designed for snowboarders. Period. There's no halfway-house design for people outside the sport. "M3 only wants to talk to snow-boarders," says Doug. "In fact, the site pushes navigation and the general experience in such a way that people who don't know snowboarding and aren't adventurous are likely to get confused, frustrated and even seriously pissed off. There's no translation for non-snowboarders, no index to make sure they find all the little hidden goodies, and no hand holding through a rather mysterious — yet consistent — navigation system."

Over the three years that Paris France has produced sites for M3, the agency has regularly created a sense of mystery to bring people back to the site. "By forcing people to discover what the site has to offer, rather than laying everything out, people have to come back to see if they've found everything." says Doug. Last year, M3 made return users a big priority; a challenge that Paris France met by feeding in content at regular intervals and releasing interviews over the course of the year.

By deliberately creating a place that interests the core audience, yet frustrates outsiders, Paris France has solidified the community aspect of M3's brand. "With the Web, we're not just communicating a message, we're creating an experience that stands for the brand," says Doug. "And it has to be an experience the target audience wants. Snowboarders like the fact this is made just for them and no one else." Like the boards themselves, the M3 site is designed for riders by riders.

PULL

www.nationalgeographic.com/pearlharbor

CLIENT: National Geographic

DESIGNED BY: Second Story

SIZE OF PROJECT TEAM: 9 people

DEVELOPMENT TIME: 3 months

TECHNOLOGY USED: ActionScript, database, Flash, HTML and Javascript

CONTACT: www.secondstory.com

"The National Geographic brand represents research and exploration. The experience of using the map is one in which users explore the various presentations to piece together the sequence of events that defined our entrance into World War II"

IN COMMEMORATING PEARL HARBOR, SECOND STORY CREATED AN ATTACK MAP THAT COMBINED BOTH NATIONAL GEOGRAPHIC'S PENCHANT FOR RESEARCH AND ITS SENSE OF EXPLORATION

On 7 December 1941 — "The day that will live in infamy," as President Roosevelt called it — scores of Japanese planes attacked the US fleet in Pearl Harbor, Hawaii, bringing the country into the Second World War and changing the face of the conflict.

To commemorate Pearl Harbor's 60th anniversary, the National Geographic Society decided to launch an evolving site that would bring together audio, video, still imagery, maps, animations and first-person accounts in its recreation of that historic day.

In addition to fitting in smoothly with the society's overall portfolio, the site needed a unique feature that would serve National Geographic's more specific online initiative. The solution, as Portland-based creators Second Story discovered, was an "Attack Map" — an interactive device that would bring the story to life. "The National Geographic brand represents research and exploration,"

Second Story's "Attack Map" brings the story of Pearl Harbor to life.

PEARL HARBOR ATTACK MAP

WAYNE CISSNA ★ U.S. SAILOR

water, and the torpedoes go right under her and into the side of the *Arizona*. But what got the *Arizona* was a bomb. It apparently went right down the stack beside the ammunition hold. And the ammunition holds just blew up."

"I swear—that's the most awe-inspiring sight I've ever seen. To see that much metal in a stream, going up—about three hundred feet I guess it went up."

0810 Overview

U.S.S. Arizona explodes
Photograph courtesy National Archives, photo no. 80-G-06683

We Were There...

Wayne Cissna
U.S. Sailor

TURN MUSIC OFF

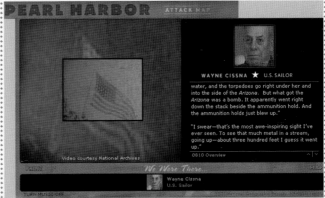

PEARL HARBOR ATTACK MAP

WAYNE CISSNA ★ U.S. SAILOR

water, and the torpedoes go right under her and into the side of the *Arizona*. But what got the *Arizona* was a bomb. It apparently went right down the stack beside the ammunition hold. And the ammunition holds just blew up."

"I swear—that's the most awe-inspiring sight I've ever seen. To see that much metal in a stream, going up—about three hundred feet I guess it went up."

0810 Overview

Video courtesy National Archives

We Were There...

Wayne Cissna
U.S. Sailor

TURN MUSIC OFF

NATIONALGEOGRAPHIC.COM

HOME | SEARCH | GET E-MAIL UPDAT

Remembering PEARL HARBOR ATTACK MAP

O A H U

ZOOM

U.S.S. Condor

MINESWEEPER SPOTS SUBMARINE PERISCOPE. FULL STORY

0342 hours - U.S. Navy minesweeper *Condor* sights periscope.

0300 0400 0500 0600 0700 0800 0900 1000 1100 1200 1300

TURN MUSIC OFF

© 2001 National Geographic Society. All rights reserved

PHOTO OF THE DAY ▶
Click here!
NATIONALGEOGRAPHIC.COM

HOME | ATTACK MAP
MEMORY BOOK
MUSEUM STORE
HISTORY | CREDITS

▶▶ OUT THERE ⊗ TOYOTA

Discovery lies at the heart of the Pearl Harbor website; users can control how fast they move from one significant event to the next.

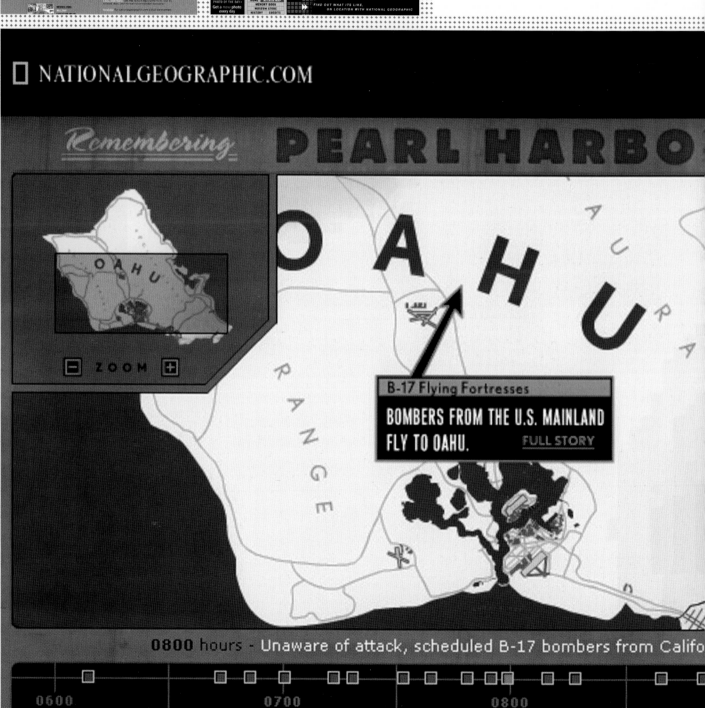

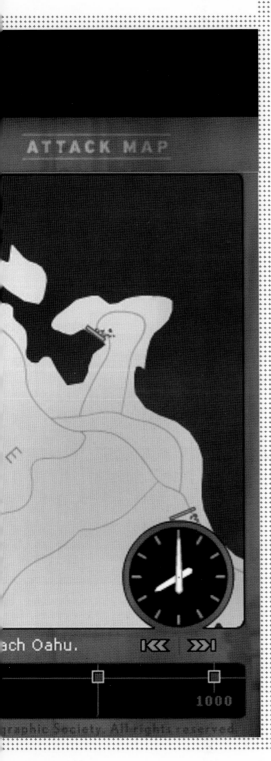

ATTACK MAP

ach Oahu.

1000

says Julie Beeler, co-founder of Second Story. "The experience of using the map is one in which users explore the various presentations to piece together the sequence of events that defined our entrance into World War II."

Discovery lies at the heart of the Attack Map's existence; users can control how fast they move from one significant event to the next, and can tilt and rotate the view — changing the perspective from which they understand the story. The map, created as isometric vector line art to enable this scaling and rotation, starts zoomed out with Japan and the US both visible, then zooms into Hawaii, and then further still into Pearl Harbor. It is at this point that users can pan the map using a timeline tool that contextualizes the geographical and historical information into one interface. The information is displayed as

a variety of newsreel-style reports, battle details and first-person survivor accounts, which appear at different milestone keyframes throughout the attack.

It is this variety of detailed information presentation that helps infuse the map with an aura of qualified research and authority, typical of the National Geographic brand. For the first-person accounts, Second Story hired the film-maker David Waingarten to find and interview survivors in order to bring the milestones to life, and, ultimately, to share these with visitors to the site in the context of the actual battle. "Because Flash can stream high-quality audio, we were able to include extended narrative segments from these men, without having to pop up some sort of external player," says Julie. "The audio starts playing immediately, while the animated imagery appears, showing scenes from the attack."

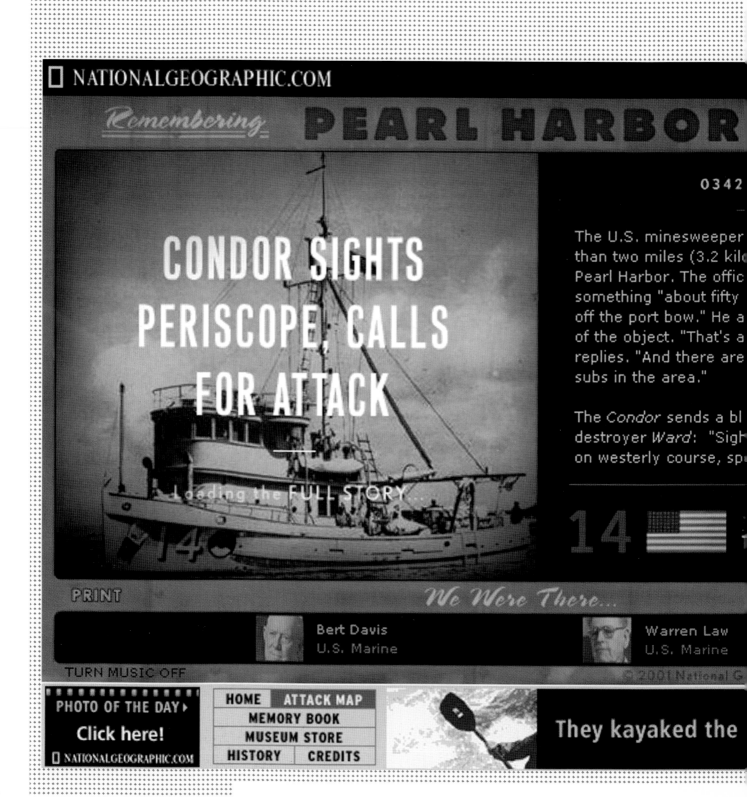

Remembering **PEARL HARBOR**

0342

CONDOR SIGHTS PERISCOPE, CALLS FOR ATTACK

—

Loading the FULL STORY...

The U.S. minesweeper
than two miles (3.2 kilo
Pearl Harbor. The offic
something "about fifty
off the port bow." He a
of the object. "That's a
replies. "And there are
subs in the area."

The *Condor* sends a bl
destroyer *Ward*: "Sigh
on westerly course, spe

14

PRINT

We Were There...

Bert Davis
U.S. Marine

Warren Law
U.S. Marine

TURN MUSIC OFF

© 2001 National G

HOME | ATTACK MAP
MEMORY BOOK
MUSEUM STORE
HISTORY | CREDITS

They kayaked the

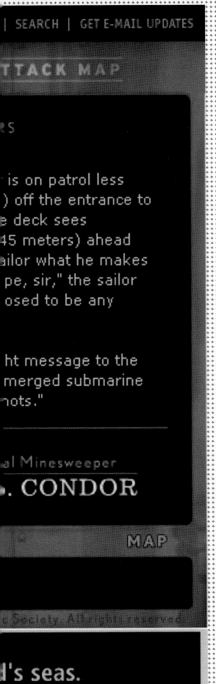

TTACK MAP

R S

is on patrol less
) off the entrance to
 deck sees
45 meters) ahead
ailor what he makes
pe, sir," the sailor
osed to be any

ht message to the
merged submarine
hots."

al Minesweeper

. CONDOR

MAP

d's seas.

The very personal nature of
these accounts is balanced
by the site's newsreel-style
reports. Second Story also
altered the quality of the
audio to enhance its
authenticity, adding a crystal
mic effect during recording,
and then dialling in the
sound effect using mp3
compression in Flash. "With
all National Geographic
modules, we have the
opportunity to create a look
and feel that's appropriate
to the content of the project,"
says Julie. "We carry the
National Geographic logo as
an overall identifier, but
that's about it as far as
branding elements go. Rather,
we create an interactive
experience that promotes the
National Geographic brand in
a unique way."

www.nikewomen.com

CLIENT: Nike

DESIGNED BY: Framfab

DEVELOPMENT TIME: Ongoing

SIZE OF PROJECT TEAM: N/A

TECHNOLOGY USED: Flash, HTML, Java and Unix

CONTACT: www.framfab.dk

"Sparring with the client is probably the most important element. It works much better than retiring to your world and shutting your client out until you've invented your version of their brand"

SPEAK
THE
TRUTH

THINK YOU KNOW IT ALL?
THINK AGAIN. DRAG THE ICONS
TO HER MOUTH FOR FACTS
YOU NEVER KNEW.

ABS

AIR GLARE

ALARM CLOCK

©NIKE Retail Services, Inc. 1999-2001

nike.com

FRAMFAB'S·NIKE·WOMEN·SITE·ADDS·A·FEMALE·PERSPECTIVE TO·THE·NIKE·ATTITUDE·IN·A·BID·TO·BUILD·A·LONG—TERM RELATIONSHIP·BETWEEN·THE·AUDIENCE·AND·THE·BRAND

Professional sport is a male-dominated domain. In the US, the women's basketball league has only recently formed — some 50 years after the NBA was established. The English Football Association boasts 92 men's football teams but only one women's squad. PGA Tour winners pocket more than their LPGA counterparts, and it's the same story on both the tennis and the athletic circuits. Step down a level, though, and it's a very different proposition — just as many women enrol at gyms, compete at weekends or pound the streets in an effort to stay fit.

Danish agency Framfab's Nike Women site exists for these women. It's a continuation of an offline campaign that introduced a new line of apparel and trainers. "The new line was designed for performance with the athletic woman in mind," says Bettina Sherain, Framfab's key account manager. "It's designed for women by women."

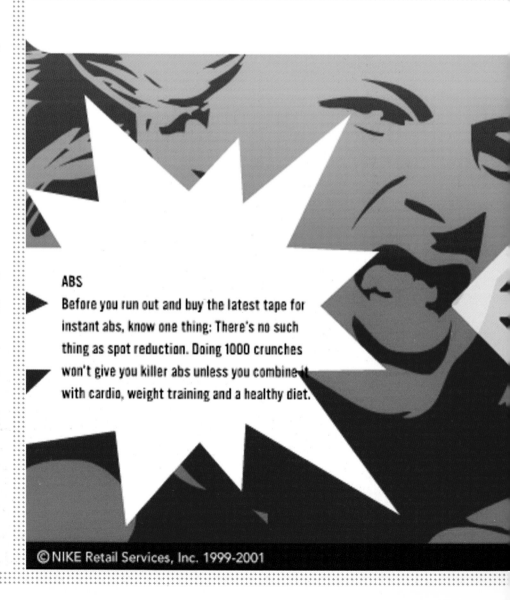

ABS
Before you run out and buy the latest tape for instant abs, know one thing: There's no such thing as spot reduction. Doing 1000 crunches won't give you killer abs unless you combine it with cardio, weight training and a healthy diet.

© NIKE Retail Services, Inc. 1999-2001

nikewomen.com

BIRTHDAY CAKE

FROWN

ABS

AIR GLARE

THINK YOU KNOW IT ALL?
THINK AGAIN. DRAG THE ICONS
TO HER MOUTH FOR FACTS
YOU NEVER KNEW.

nike.com

In developing nikewomen.com, Framfab used a
combination of direct, insightful and humorous
content with a female appeal in order to establish an
ongoing relationship with its audience.

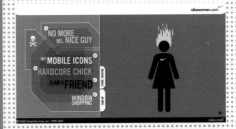

Despite targeting sporty
women consumers, Nike Women
follows the same brand
attitude as Nike itself.
It is not a separate brand,
but a brand extension.
However, a specific market
requires a specific approach.
Framfab decided to use a
combination of direct,
insightful and humorous
content with a female appeal
in order to establish an
ongoing relationship with its
audience. Users can join
debates, search for events,
or browse for merchandise.

Building up a rapport with
the audience over time is
a key part of the brand's
infiltration into the users'
daily lives. Framfab
recognizes that the audience
isn't going to immediately
embrace a brand, no matter
how well known it might be.
It takes time and the
continual assertion of
relevant brand values to
develop such a strong bond.
For this reason, the Nike
Women site is continually
updated. So far, there have
been four new sites — all
launched to coincide with
offline campaigns — in Nike's

The **Nike Women** site is continually updated, as part
of an ongoing assertion of its brand values.

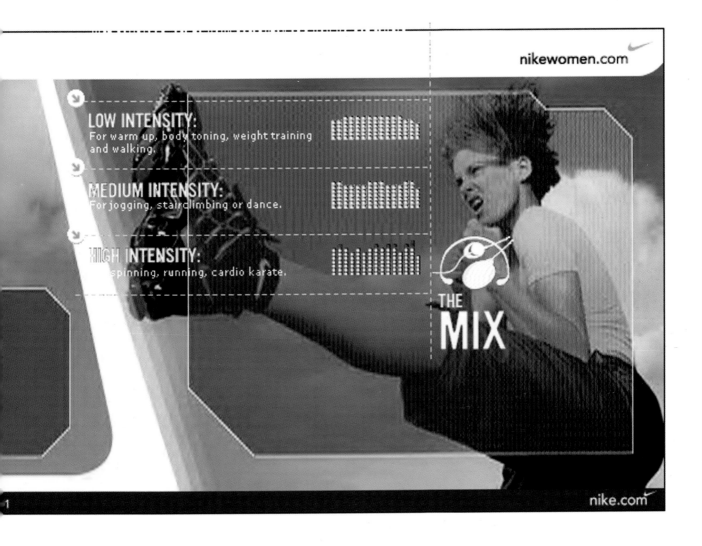

nikewomen.com

LOW INTENSITY:
For warm up, body toning, weight training and walking.

MEDIUM INTENSITY:
For jogging, stairclimbing or dance.

HIGH INTENSITY:
Spinning, running, cardio karate.

THE
MIX

nike.com

aim to establish itself as
a relevant brand for the
athletic woman.

In Framfab's way of working,
the same reasoning applies
to the relationship between
agency and brand. "Under-
standing a brand happens over
time, and good results are
achieved when you work very
closely with your clients,"
says Bettina. "Sparring is
probably the most important
element and it works much
better than retiring to your
world and shutting your client
out until you've invented
your version of their brand.
Working with Nike, we came to
appreciate the Nike brand as
an amalgam of many different
things: the constant striving
to stay true to sports, the
belief that if you have a
body, you are an athlete,
and the 'Just Do It' pay-off.
In its marketing, Nike is
audacious and irreverent. We
designed the Nike Women site
with the same attitude, but
with an added female
perspective."

www·volkswagenasia·com

CLIENT: Volkswagen Asia Pacific

DESIGNED BY: Bluewave Singapore

DEVELOPMENT TIME: 3 months

SIZE OF PROJECT TEAM: 7 people

TECHNOLOGY USED: ActionScript, Flash, Generator, HTML, JavaScript, JSP and Photoshop

CONTACT: www·bluewave·com

"We wanted to take the very latest Internet tools and applications and use them to reflect how innovative Volkswagen was in creating its cars"

INNOVATE/TECH.

Lifestyle

Environment

Safety

Creativity

Provocative and Exhilarating Concept Car
New Beetle Dune

A Beetle Study that's aimed directly at the needs of **sport-oriented** people.

BLUEWAVE•SINGAPORE•USED•THE•LATEST
INTERNET•TECHNOLOGY•TO•CONVEY•VOLKSWAGEN'S
INNOVATIVE•NATURE•TO•ITS•NEW•AUDIENCE

please selec

Some Volk

This is due

please select a car to visualise:

new beetle golf variant bora sharan lupa
polo golf cabrio golf passat passat varia

r model

models are not available.
lability in your chosen country.

When Bluewave won the Volkswagen Asia Pacific account, it faced two immediate problems. Firstly, as a new brand in Asia, Volkswagen had very little recognition. Secondly, the company had even less of an online identity. In fact, the Volkswagen Asia site was its first exposure to the Internet.

"We wanted to take the very latest Internet tools and applications and use them to reflect how innovative Volkswagen was in creating its cars," says Chris Elkin, Bluewave's project manager on the Volkswagen site. Bluewave's initial aims were to enhance the understanding of Volkswagen in Asia and make sure that people came to associate innovation and sophistication with the company. The development of a section called the "Faces of Volkswagen", which built up the pan-Asian presence of Volkswagen by detailing the company's heritage and where it was heading, addressed the first issue. The Visualiser took care of the second.

Designed like a software tool, the Visualiser is an interactive car-building system that enables users

As a new brand in Asia, Volkswagen had no associations for people on the continent. Bluewave used the latest Internet tools to reflect Volkswagen's innovative nature.

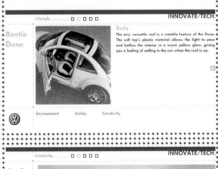

to construct their own Volkswagen, dragging and dropping their chosen engine, colour, fabric and extras into the model of their choice. "The Visualiser pushes at the extremes of Volkswagen's core brand values," says Chris. "It doesn't give the customer a dream car — it gives them an innovative tool that they can play with and create their ideal car that Volkswagen can deliver. It's got a VW laboratory feel to it; you construct your own car almost as the Volkswagen technician in Berlin would."

Channelling users can be tricky, especially with cars, where the cost is a little higher than the books sites such as Amazon deal in. This is where the Visualiser comes in. "The Visualiser is a one-to-one interactive tool that gets people to interact with the brand and then gets them into the dealers, where they can really get the whole Volkswagen experience," says Chris. No prices are displayed on the website, so users have to go into the showroom if they want to continue the experience.

Bluewave has turned VW Asia into the complete selling tool: an experience that pushes the brand, gives detailed information on the product in an interactive way and, in a final touch often ignored by other car manufacturers' sites, enables users to carry on through to their local dealers and make a purchase. Once users have built their ideal car, they have two choices. Going straight through to their dealership means that the whole brand experience is taken right to its logical conclusion. And, thanks to the Visualiser, the dealer is already in possession of their specific details. The other option — getting the URL emailed to their desktop — keeps the relationship with Volkswagen Asia going offline. "It's a great way of getting back on people's computers, into their inboxes and in front of their eyes," says Willem Mulder, Bluewave's creative director. Even if you resist temptation on your first visit, Volkswagen will get you in the end.

Models

Visualiser

Faces of
Volkswagen

History

Awards

Press Releases

Owner's Club

Dealer
Locator

Importers

Service
Request

Innovate
/Tech.

New Beetle

The Visualiser is a one-to-one tool that gets people to interact with the brand as they create their ideal car.

Faces of Volkswagen

History   Awards   Press Releases   Owner's Club

34 - 39   45 - 50   57 - 61   65 - 72   77 - 84   92 - 98
     40 - 44   50 - 56   62 - 64   73 - 76   85 - 91

On examining the birth and development of the Volkswagen Group -- today one of the world's largest motor vehicle manufacturers -- it becomes clear just how closely the history of the company is bound up with the contemporary history of Germany. The unique circumstances in which Volkswagen developed make its history more than just a fascinating account of the evolution from the Beetle to the current model range; it is a reflection of the development of a whole society.

With this in mind, this chronicle does not simply list dates, facts, development and production figures, but aims to flesh out the by now well-known official history with behind-the-scenes stories and reports and a dash of authentic atmosphere.

The following pages describe what Volkswagen once was, and what it is today. We hope that you will gain pleasure and enjoyment from this chronicle.

Asia Pacific

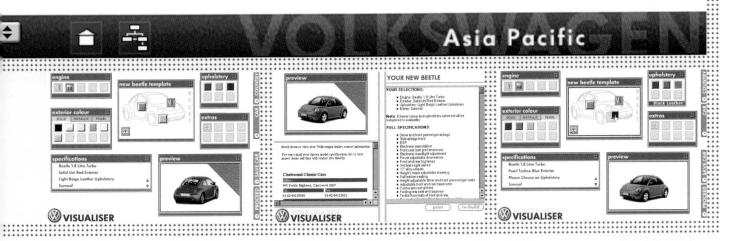

www.wallpaper.com

CLIENT: Wallpaper*
DESIGNED BY: I-D Media
DEVELOPMENT TIME: 4 months
SIZE OF PROJECT TEAM: 6 people
TECHNOLOGY USED: Flash 5, Photoshop and PHP
CONTACT: www.i-dmedia.com

"A lot of brands overdo their sites. A minimalist approach often gives users a better understanding of the brand"

wallpaper*

I-D·MEDIA·PLAYED·ON·EMOTIVE·AND·STRUCTURAL ASSOCIATIONS·TO·BRING·WALLPAPER*'S·STRONG IDENTITY·IN·PRINT·ONLINE

There's an old Web design adage that states you should never transfer your print work to the Internet and that online design is a whole new ball game which, therefore, requires a totally different approach. So, what happens when your brief is to do exactly that: to recreate online the essence of one of the strongest magazine brands on the market today?

When I-D Media started work on Wallpaper.com, it decided to play on these offline associations. It wanted users to feel like they were virtually flicking through the magazine when they visited the site. "We were after the same sort of emotive feeling you get when you flip through the magazine itself," says Shalini Bharadwaj, a senior designer at I-D Media. "All the images move from right to left as you navigate through the sections. It's about keeping the illustrative style and sensitivity of reading the real thing."

Wallpaper* is very much a style-led creation; it is strong in what it says and how it presents information. Leafing through half a dozen copies of the magazine was enough to give the agency a detailed insight into Wallpaper*'s corporate and magazine culture. "Wallpaper* is a pretty unique brand; it's kind of like a piece of art in itself," says Merle Busch, key account manager at I-D Media. "It's not a magazine where the focus is just on the content. There's a lot of quality design work that has to be transferred online as well."

Bringing the visual impression of the magazine to life online was one part of the project, but I-D Media decided to go beyond what was already implicit in Wallpaper*'s brand. "We wanted to create an online brand that was an addition to the magazine and not just a total copy," says Merle. The agency decided on the concept of reducing the site

wallpaper*

MUNICHNAVIGATOR

PLACES TO STAY

PLACES TO EAT

PLACES TO DRINK

PLACES TO SHOP

PLACES TO VISIT

TEN THINGS YOU MUST DO

FIVE BEER HALLS & GARDENS

USEFUL NUMBERS

004

TRAVEL

I-D Media wanted users to feel like they were virtually flicking through the magazine when they visited the Wallpaper site. The illustrative style remains the same, and images move from right to left as you navigate through the sections.

wallpaper*

002 SPACE

Urban anthropology, interior views and definitive domains

002 WALLPAPERHOUSEURBANADDITION
OPENHOUSECONCEPTHOUSE   icollector.com

SPACE

wallpaper*

NEW YORK ICFF

New York's International Contemporary Furniture Fair has positioned itself as the best America has to offer. Suzy Hoodless and Becky Jones report on this year's sta and stripes from the home of the brave

001 NEWSW*DISPATCH
NEWYORKICFF

INTELLIGENCE

wallpaper*

001 NEWSW*DISPATCH
NEWYORKICFF

BESTOFSHOW INSITE
OUTOFSITERESOURCES

INTELLIGENCE   A D I

to a strip of wallpaper that
runs across the page, within
which all the content is
presented. Copy on the site
also implements the spirit
of the magazine, whether
it's taken directly from
the offline magazine or is
individually commissioned
content.

As well as making sure it
carried the same style of
content, I-D Media also
developed the site's
navigation experience to
reflect Wallpaper*'s image.
"Wallpaper* didn't deserve
the traditional approach of
taking its users by the hand
and leading them through
every part of the site," says
Merle. "The navigation needed
to be more adventurous. It
needed to be more of an
unusual way of interpreting
the Wallpaper* brand." The
non-linear navigation I-D
Media finally settled on fits
in with the artistic style of
Wallpaper*, and enables
people to come back to the
site and find something new
each time.

Wallpaper.com's adventurous non-linear navigation fits in
with the artistic style of the magazine, and enables people
to come back to the site and find something new each time.

wallpaper*

ITALIAN MUSCLE ▶

With powerhouse firms like **B&B Italia**, **Alivar** and **Luminaire** exhibiting for the first time, the ICFF earned its place on the international design circuit in 2000. The Italian contingent swelled to double last year's number and made its presence felt by taking up almost a quarter of

▶

001 NEWSW*DISPATCH
NEWYORKICFF

INTELLIGENCE

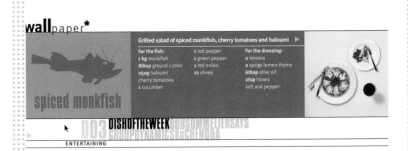

With much of the work on
wallpaper.com detailed to
reflect the emotive and
structural image of the
brand, the key to the site's
identity is its understated
presentation. "A lot of
brands make the mistake of
overdoing their sites,"
says Kevin Dowd, head of
interactive development at
I-D Media. "I believe that
less is more. An online
brand can be destroyed if
the designers start playing
around with the look and
feel too much. It can make
it tough for users to find
the content they're looking
for. The message has to be
clear, and a minimalist
approach can often give users
a better understanding of the
brand." With Wallpaper*'s
subtle design and structural
branding, less is definitely
more.

www.wmteam.de

SITE: WM Team

DESIGNED BY: WM Team

DEVELOPMENT TIME: 2 months

SIZE OF PROJECT TEAM: 4 people

TECHNOLOGY USED: Flash, Freehand, Image Ready, LightWave, Photoshop and Swift 3D

CONTACT: www.wmteam.de

"The most important thing for us was to give our brand a unique position; to do something that people wouldn't expect. Being different gives people something to talk about"

DESIGNING▪YOUR▪OWN▪SITE▪IS▪NOTORIOUSLY▪DIFFICULT.
GERMAN▪AGENCY▪WM▪TEAM▪COMBINED▪DESIGN▪WITH
PERSONALITY▪TO▪EXPRESS▪ITS▪OWN▪UNIQUE▪BRAND

WM Team wanted its site to express the company's fun-loving attitude and tight-knit structure.

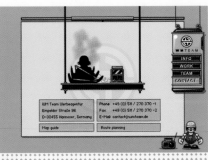

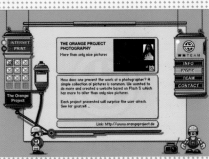

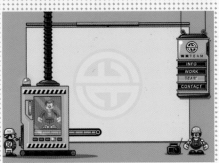

WM Team's site is full of humorous touches that help build the company's fun-loving character and tight-knit team structure.

WM Team is an agency site apart. Its different approach was key to the company's aim of giving its brand a unique position.

It's your shop window. Your showcase to the world. A chance to woo potential clients with your creative skills and your working culture. It's your agency's own website. And it matters. Big time.

Clients might approach a design agency on the strength of its existing portfolio, but it's often their own site that ties the deal. To this extent, your own site needs to say who you are, how you operate, what you can do and, above all, why you're worthy of the project. In essence, it needs to reflect your overall brand.

German agency WM Team has got it pretty much nailed. An online advertising agency with a strong competence in Flash design, Hanover-based WM Team wanted its site to express the company's fun-loving attitude and tight-knit structure, alongside the usual suspects such as

news, portfolio and contact details. "Every company needs a design that fits its philosophy," says WM Team's art director Rainer Michael. "We believe that advertising should be fun and entertaining, but with a strong sense of interactivity and functionality. Our aim is to get well known for this kind of Web design."

WM Team started out looking for a "story" for the site and experimented with various ideas in search of a narrative vehicle. In the end, the designers decided they were trying to be too clever, and settled on using little workers to build up the site as you progress through the pages. The hard-hatted characters load up WM Team's client portfolio, introduce users to Rainer and his colleagues, and generally tinker about the site — enhanced throughout with subtle, character-building touches. "We like to work for customers with courage," says Rainer. "If a company wants to be noticed, it has to take a different approach and that's what we did. Using little builders creates an entertaining atmosphere, as well as effectively reflecting the idea of 'teamwork'."

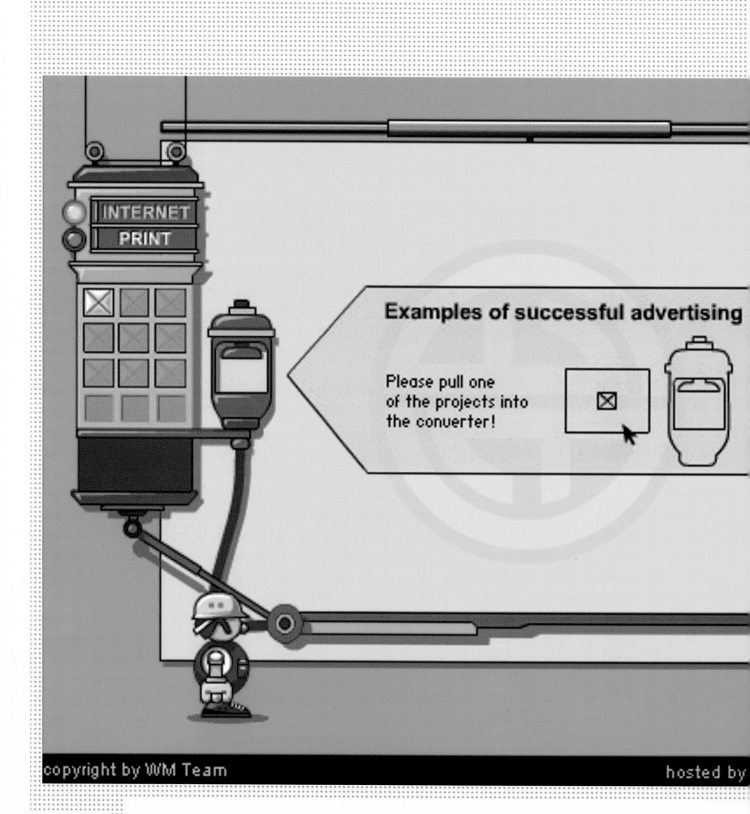

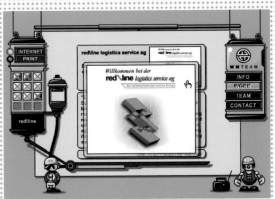

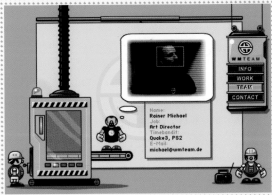

The wmteam.de site won an Orange Rubber Arrow award – the Web design equivalent of an Oscar – in the Motion Graphics category at Flashforward New York.

Unlike the majority of websites, agency sites don't rely on traffic regularly returning to pay their bills. If their own site does enough to attract a handful of clients, then its job is done. Therefore, a site with personality, a site that reflects the brand and sticks in people's minds, is going to have a more lasting effect than a more traditional approach. "We don't have to bring people back; there's no changing content on our site," explains Rainer. "But it is important that people have got to know us by the time they leave the site — and that they keep us in mind."

Awareness of WM Team's site took on a new level when it picked up an Orange Rubber Arrow — the Web-design equivalent of an Oscar — in the Motion Graphics category at Flashforward New York. A nice way of proving WM Team's approach to advertising and design worked, the award also confirmed the agency's strong online brand. "The most important thing for us was to give our brand a unique position; to do something that people wouldn't expect," says Rainer. "Being different gives people something to talk about." And word travels fast.

GUIDE▪TO▪
ONLINE▪BRANDING

"Brands are ephemeral. You should really be able to experience them with your eyes closed," says Digit's Toby Evetts. Good online branding does this. There's certainly a big difference between translating the look of a brand and its spirit, and the 15 case studies in this book have not only achieved the first but, more importantly, the latter as well. They are by no means the definitive list on how to approach branding, but they are a source of inspiration and a roll-call of ways of doing it. The key is to learn from these creative approaches. The variables of each project will obviously differ depending on what suits the brand, its audience and its online objectives. There are, however, a few rules worth bearing in mind that will help.

1.UNDERSTAND▪THE▪BRAND

Slick design and an innovative experience count for nothing if the essence of the brand is not understood. Failure to grasp its values, appeal and position in the marketplace will result in a failing online venture. "It's very important to go with the design of the offline brand, but it's much more important to understand the brand itself," says I-D Media's Merle Busch.

"The most important thing is to know the brand and to drive it down through every point of contact," agrees Scient's Tomas Ancona. "It's not just at the front door, it's every touch point — be it tone of content, navigational structure or the visual language that runs all the way through the site. Your customer experience is your brand."

Everything that goes into a site's production — the way it's designed, the technology used, the experience offered — should be in keeping with the brand. Even the style of using the site should reflect its character. "Usability is now much more about understanding the brand; understanding what experiences you should have and how they should match that brand," says Deepend's Jane Austen. "The Sony site, www.scee.com, is almost impossible to use but its target market love it — there are little mouse-overs, hidden information and secret sections that are just right for PlayStation users."

Numerous client meetings and brand workshops will provide an insight into the brand, but the best way to fully understand it is by carrying out careful research. Some projects may not enjoy this luxury, but it is key to carry out research with as many different people as possible. When Digit took on the Habitat site, it canvassed the people who had already worked with Habitat: the agencies, the design company, the publishers of the catalogue, the technical team, the marketing department — the entire network of associates. It also approached the manager of the Tottenham Court Road store in London and even the sofa buyer; anyone who could provide another insight into the company. "A lot of important issues came out of that, not least the things that were frustrating Habitat's customers," says Digit's Toby Evetts. "It gave us a lot of information that, while not immediately applicable to the design, was very important in helping us solve these issues." The central product database on the Habitat site was a direct result of these conversations.

2. KNOW YOUR AUDIENCE

Once a good understanding of the brand has been developed, familiarity with the target market will have been achieved as well. However, knowing how the brand wants to portray itself is a different proposition from knowing what the audience actually wants.

"You really need to have an understanding of who the audience is and what their culture is about," says Juxt Interactive's Todd Purgason. "You need to ask yourself what your audience is looking for, what they need, and how you can use the Internet to supply that need." When I-D Media developed its site for Wallpaper*, it specifically created an adventurous form of non-linear navigation to appeal to the magazine's design-conscious audience. Likewise, Rufus Leonard's site for Mercedes-Benz UK recognizes the difference in needs between Mercedes's van customers and its more traditional consumers in the car market.

Depending on who the audience is, branding will also play a stronger or weaker role than the content, so the branding process will vary project by project. Some will require a more specific treatment than others, where the level of branding varies depending on the audience, the experience and the brief.

3. PROVIDE A SERVICE

Good online brands, like good offline brands, set themselves apart by enhancing their users' lives in some way. Online branding succeeds when a service is provided. "You have to deliver some kind of value to your user," says Guardian Unlimited's Chris Moisan. "You have to entertain people, help them save time or waste time, save money or spend money. Boo.com is a classic example of what happens when you don't. Boo had a beautiful design and the concept was great, but the brand died because the site was so difficult to use."

Banja and Habitat are good examples of sites that provide their users with a service. Banja immerses its users in an online game and makes them feel constantly part of a bigger picture. Habitat, on the other hand, enables its customers to do some virtual decorating. The "MyHabitat" section lets users drag in their products and play with background, size, colour and texture to find out what products they want before spending any money.

4. USE THE MEDIUM

The most common Web design mistakes arise from people not understanding the Internet as a design medium. The Web gives users the chance to interact with brands on a personal level — a powerful tool that a lot of sites don't maximize.

Bluewave developed an innovative application on its Volkswagen Asia site that would have been impossible to produce in any other branding medium. Being able to construct their own car in the Visualiser gets people to interact with the brand on a very immersive level. Essentially, they're doing the same job as Volkswagen's Berlin technicians. Likewise, Habitat's 'MyHabitat' application, previously noted for its service provision, is an ideal online tool.

Slick design and an
innovative experience count
for nothing if the essence of
the brand is not understood

5, MAKE IT CONSISTENT

The greater the number of people that come into contact with a brand, the more its meaning gets fortified. Consistency in branding is, therefore, vital. The same message and values must be delivered across the whole site, across all sites and across all media.

"Getting consistency throughout the whole site is crucial," says Imagination's David Chamberlain. "You have to make sure that even minor details still remain similar; that there's not one point that will let it down. It's the same when you're working with a multinational that has a number of regional sites. We did a survey for Ford a couple of years ago where we took screenshots of its various sites around the world and put them together on one page. The difference was incredible. It's all very well having separate identities for different products, but somewhere along the line something's got to be sufficiently consistent to enable users to build their relationship with the brand."

Achieving consistency across a variety of websites counts for nothing if the TV campaign is delivering a different message. The site experience needs to be entirely concordant with what the brand is trying to do in other media. "Online branding needs to be consistent with any other expression of branding, be it print, radio or TV," says Levi Strauss's Anne Bonew. "These things just don't work in isolation."

Without a standard message, users will quickly become confused as to what the brand stands for. Websites suffer when their layout, theme or experience is discrepant with people's brand associations. According to the team at Digit, airlines do it very badly. "British Airways has spent a lot of time and energy on its site, but you just don't get the experience of the brand," says Digit's Rob Cooke. "You don't get this feeling that it's got the most incredible infrastructure in the world to get you from A to B. It's not a reflective experience because of the way that you navigate through the device online, and it has an effect on the brand. People don't blame the design company or the brand manager, they blame the brand itself, and it's such a competitive marketplace that they will just click off."

6. EARN THEIR TRUST

If you have followed the previous five rules, your users should start to trust your online brand. There are, however, a few more ways of establishing your brand's reputation. Firstly, make sure you keep your promises. Amazon has established itself as one of the few strong Internet brands because, in addition to catering for its audience, it works hard to ensure its goods reach you as and when it originally stated. This applies just as much to the smaller details on your site. If a link says it will connect people to a product search, make sure that it does. Make sure that all fulfilment points on the site — comments, registration, etc — are successful.

Secondly, exceed your audience's expectations. Provide them with what they were anticipating and then add on that little bit extra. "People are less likely to go and visit a brand offline if it can't offer them what they want online," says Good Technology's Xanthe Arvanitakis. "You have to meet their expectations, in fact better their expectations, give them something to really be surprised about" Fulfil your audience's needs and then some. If they sit up and take notice of your brand, then guess where they'll be heading the next time they're online.

The Web gives users the chance to
interact with brands on a personal
level — a powerful tool that a lot
of sites don't maximize

THE FUTURE OF
BRAND DEVELOPMENT

So, where next for online branding? Onwards, upwards and outwards, according to lookandfeel's Charlie O'Shields. "Online branding could become the central vehicle for brand delivery," he says. "Once companies start utilizing the Internet to its full potential, we will see more 'brand communities'. Major brands will look for ways to deliver their message in a truly interactive and immersive format that urges users to 'come together and share', creating a bond not only between the consumer and the brand, but also between consumers themselves. With the community approach, companies will be able to increase brand loyalty, as the consumers will become more aware of other users who share their brand interest."

As the Internet continues to advance, more applications will arise to push and evolve the way branding is approached. The advent of interactive TV and 3G mobile phones bodes well for cross-platform branding, while one-to-one marketing and personalization continue to be central to the future of online branding.

Cross-platforming — developing a channel brand strategy that builds up a puzzle of the brand - depends on the individual brand that you are dealing with, though. "Even if the brand itself is strong, it doesn't make sense to try and move into every new field," says I-D Media's Merle Busch. "You have to ask yourself where the medium is going and if the platform really fits the brand." When Deepend finished its site for Conran, it dismissed instantly expanding into other media. "Conran is a very traditionally minded company, so it would almost be off-brand for it to do something with WAP technology," says Deepend's Nicky Gibson. "And the demographics of iDTV probably wouldn't suit Conran's audience either."

As for the next step for online branding itself, one-to-one marketing and personalization are hot topics at the moment. In fact, they've been hot topics for a while. One-to-one marketing on any sizeable scale is little more than a pipe dream at the moment — technology and perceptions of privacy currently prevent otherwise. However, opinion is divided as to whether they will truly transform the way we approach online branding. Martin Lindstrom, author of Brand Building on the Internet, thinks they will. "One-to-one marketing will change the role of brands, as they will move from a position where they were just talking, to one where they also have to listen, learn and react," he says. "If they don't react, then people will just move away from them."

Others are not so enthusiastic, though. "We all talk about one-to-one marketing a lot, but what's one-to-one marketing and what's intrusion?" says Good Technology's Xanthe Arvanitakis. It's a fine line between the two and Xanthe's view has been backed up by the formation of the Online Privacy Alliance, a trade group of 50 large American companies including America Online, AT&T and Procter & Gamble, whose task it is to self-regulate online marketing before the US government does it for them.

Intrusion aside, questions remain over its usefulness. Many think that one-to-one marketing is too restrictive. Things change, even during the same day, and people aren't defined by their data but by their attitudes. Levi's Anne Bonew sums it up best when she says: "One-to-one marketing and personalization are only tools to be used if it's appropriate for the brand. And if you do use them, well, you'd better make sure that everything about them reflects your brand values."

Whatever the future for online branding, one thing's for sure. It's here to stay. The dotcom crash taught us a few hard-learnt lessons, but agencies have come out stronger and wiser. Strong offline brands and innovative start-ups with sound business models are picking up the lead. Get under the skin of the brand, know the audience, use the medium effectively and consistently, and online brands will flourish.

LAURENCE KING

Published in 2002 by Laurence King Publishing Ltd
71 Great Russell Street
London WC1B 3BP
TEL: + 44 20 7430 8850
FAX: + 44 20 7430 8880
E-MAIL: enquiries@laurenceking.co.uk
www.laurenceking.co.uk

Copyright 2002 Laurence King Publishing Ltd

A catalogue record for this book
is available from the British Library.

ISBN: 1 85669 294 9

Printed in Hong Kong
DESIGN: Daniel Delaney